NO TURNING BACK

NO TURNING BACK

My Summer with Daddy King

Gurdon Brewster

ORBIS BOOKS

Maryknoll, New York 10545

Founded in 1970, Orbis Books endeavors to publish works that enlighten the mind, nourish the spirit, and challenge the conscience. The publishing arm of the Maryknoll Fathers and Brothers, Orbis seeks to explore the global dimensions of the Christian faith and mission, to invite dialogue with diverse cultures and religious traditions, and to serve the cause of reconciliation and peace. The books published reflect the views of their authors and do not represent the official position of the Maryknoll Society. To learn more about Maryknoll and Orbis Books, please visit our website at www.maryknoll.com.

Library of Congress Cataloging-in-Publication Data

Brewster, Gurdon.
    No turning back : my summer with Daddy King / Gurdon Brewster.
       p.   cm.
    ISBN-13: 978-1-57075-728-0
    1. Brewster, Gurdon – Childhood and youth. 2. Atlanta (Ga.) –
Race relations – History – 20th century. 3. Civil rights movements –
Georgia – Atlanta – History – 20th century. 4. Whites – Georgia –
Atlanta – Biography. 5. Seminarians – New York (State) – New York –
Biography. 6. King, Martin Luther, 1899-1984 – Friends and associates.
7. King, Martin Luther, 1899-1984. 8. Baptists – Georgia – Atlanta –
Clergy – Biography. 9. Ebenezer Baptist Church (Atlanta, Ga.) History –
20th century. 10. Atlanta (Ga.) – Biography. I. Title.
F294.A89N425 2007
323.0973 – dc22
                                                        2007007670

This book is dedicated to

Daddy and Mrs. King,
who took me into their home for the summer, sight unseen,
as a white stranger from the North, and welcomed me;

The people of Ebenezer Baptist Church,
who, in 1961 and 1966, changed my life;

Lillian Watkins and Sarah Reed,
Ebenezer's management team,
who supported me in wonderful ways
and whose ability to "burn my ears"
made many days speed by too fast;

Esther Turner, the only white member of Ebenezer in 1961,
who befriended me and with her sense of history and wise counsel
helped me to reflect on my summer's activities;

Martha, my wife;

Ann, Mary, David, and Sarah, my children;

Elisa, Julia, Shannan, Kristyn, Jack, Gabriel, and Grace,
my grandchildren, the devoted cheerleaders of my life.

This book is also dedicated to
all of us, especially young people:
that we may remember the history of love and tears
that makes us who we are
and inspires us to imagine who we can become.

Contents

$\backsim$

Acknowledgments

I WISH TO ACKNOWLEDGE how grateful I am to Phil Wolfson, who encouraged me to keep writing, without whom this book would not have been written. He showed me once again the importance of an encourager in one's creative life.

I am extremely grateful to Robert Ellsberg, publisher of Orbis Books, whose commitment to me and this book brought these pages into print.

Many people helped me, especially Todd Manza, who, as an editor, guided me in preparing these pages; Irene Zahava, who cheered me on and helped fine-tune the manuscript; Rosie Magee, who typed my handwritten copy; Michael Pastore, who helped arrange the photographs and the manuscript; Stephen Singer, who prepared the black-and-white photographs; LeGrace Benson, Russell Bourne, John Finn, Sarah Reed, and Marion Van Soest, who made wise suggestions for the book.

I especially want to thank Martha, my wife, my devoted companion and editor, who believes in this story and who believes in me.

Prologue

IN THE SUMMER of 1961, as a young man in the middle of my seminary studies, I had the opportunity to work at the Ebenezer Baptist Church in Atlanta, where Reverend Martin Luther King Sr. and Dr. Martin Luther King Jr. were co-pastors. I spent the summer living with Reverend King Sr., popularly known as Daddy King, and Mrs. King. During that time, Dr. King Jr., who was leading the civil rights movement from his office in Atlanta, and I had extensive talks together. My experiences that summer changed my life forever.

On the day Dr. King was killed, something inside me was killed as well. After he died, I rarely spoke about my experiences to anyone. My silence might have continued had not one of my children revealed my secret to her teacher. Soon after that, I found myself speaking to the fourth-grade class on Martin Luther King Day about Dr. King and about my experiences in the civil rights movement.

" 'We shall overcome,' can we sing that song?" a boy asked, after I had shared my memories. "Let's sing," I said enthusiastically, not anticipating what this would unleash within me. As I stood in the circle of fourth-graders singing that great anthem of the movement that had bonded millions of people together during those amazing years, I was surprised to feel emotion building up inside me. Then I felt tears fill my eyes, followed immediately by the uncontrollable shudders of deep weeping. While holding the tiny hands on my left and my right, I had to stop singing. Tears streamed down my face as I gulped for air. The children looked at me in utter amazement. Had they ever seen a grown man cry?

"We'll walk hand in hand," they sang as the teacher kindly brought me a tissue to wipe my eyes. "We will walk in peace."

Caught completely off guard by my sudden burst of emotion, I was even more surprised than the children.

I had not sung that song for years, not marched arm in arm in the streets, not felt the searing hostility of white resistance or the binding love of black and white people creating a new world. Why had I been so restless for so long in the church and in the university? Why had America been so restless, so in search of a direction that combined real social change with profound spiritual compassion and commitment? Who was there to follow out into the streets, marching arm in arm for justice for the poor and the oppressed? Why had so many of us stopped singing?

I was a young man of twenty-four in 1961 when the civil rights movement was young as well. Rosa Parks, just five years and a few months before, had refused to give up her seat on the bus to a white man in that extraordinary act that began a revolution. Dr. King was emerging as a national leader and Reverend King, his father, was the well-known preacher at Ebenezer Baptist Church. I was about to have experiences that would carve themselves more deeply into my soul than I could imagine.

As I looked at those fourth-grade children through tear-filled eyes, I knew I wanted to convey something of the horror and something of the hope that had made that moment of American history so transformative. I wanted the spirit that had changed America to leap off the pages of history right into their hearts. I wanted to release the historical facts from being imprisoned in the pages of books so that one day these children would feel a cause, large or small, and give themselves to letting the oppressed of their own day go free.

Hidden in the story of my experiences was a deeper theme that slowly began to emerge for me over the years. As Daddy King and I ate breakfast together nearly every morning I pressed him with question after question about his remarkable life. Hardly did I realize that during those breakfasts it was as if I were searching for my own father, who had died ten years earlier. It was as if in uncovering the story of Daddy King's life I was learning something of what it is to be an adult son to a grown man who could have been my father's age. I was learning about how an adult man can take a younger man into his life by sharing what it is to be alive and human and bestowing immeasurable gifts of encouragement. I had no idea that my presence would mean anything to this great man, and it was only years later, when I invited him to visit Cornell University, that he revealed what I had meant to him, as well.

This writing is drawn from the letters I wrote, from the journals I kept, and above all, from my memories, which are still vivid, even though more than four decades have slipped past. My memories have been freshened by talking with people and reading books about the times, including Reverend King Sr.'s autobiography, *Daddy King*.

I used quotations around conversations to bring life to what I remember, and these conversations represent the best of my recollections of what actually was said.

The experiences that transform a nation and the experiences that transform an individual sometimes coincide and they sometimes connect. As a sheltered white man from the North I found myself in the eye of the storm that was rudely awakening a sheltered nation. Blind to the harsh realities of racial oppression and the system that generates and maintains poverty, our eyes were being opened by a transcendent vision that was shouted from the pulpits and sung in the streets, a vision of hope for black and white, for rich and poor, for all people everywhere in the nation and in the world. A seed of hope was planted in those years of struggle and transformation that makes me want to reach out to people, especially young people, and say that I believe this light of hope cannot be extinguished even in times of darkness. The seed of hope has become the tree of life.

And so we sing:

> I have decided to march for justice . . .
> I have decided to work for freedom . . .
> I have decided to live in hope . . .
> No turning back. No turning back.

1

Brewster Gets Ebenezer

I ENTERED THE ROOM, full of excitement, and sat down near the front. Soon one of the leaders of the Student Interracial Ministry at Union Theological Seminary in New York City called to order those of us who were interested in the program and opened with a few remarks. The meeting was a blur in my mind until the leader began reading the names of the churches that were expecting seminary students for the summer. "I'm looking for volunteers," he said.

When the name "Ebenezer" was called out, I shot my hand into the air. There was a moment of silence as my hand waved with determination like an inappropriately large flag planted in the middle of a mall parking lot. I dared not look behind me to see if other hands were also waving. I waited nervously, my hand vigorously telling the world of my intentions.

"Okay," the leader broke the silence. "Brewster gets Ebenezer." I nodded quietly while my heart exploded inside me. I had been assigned the Ebenezer Baptist Church!

In 1961, the pastors of the Ebenezer Baptist Church in Atlanta, Georgia, were Reverend Martin Luther King Sr. and Dr. Martin Luther King Jr. I was to be their assistant for the summer. My choice was not an accident. I had done enough homework on the civil rights movement and the role of Dr. King Jr. to know that Ebenezer was the one church where I wanted to work that summer. Ebenezer had been a leader in the struggle for social justice for decades under

Daddy King's leadership. Long before the civil rights movement, Daddy King had spoken out for the rights of black
people and the poor and had become known as a leader in
the city with a vision for how justice could become a reality
in their lives.

Rosa Parks had refused to give up her seat in the front of
a bus on December 1, 1955, only five years before I was to
go south. After leading the Montgomery bus boycott, Martin Luther King Jr. moved to Atlanta to set up the Southern
Christian Leadership Conference (SCLC) and to join his father as co-pastor at Ebenezer. He had been there for about a
year when the Student Interracial Ministry — the SIM, as it
was called — obtained an invitation to send a white student
into his church. I was to be one of eight white students who
were to do summer work in various black churches around
the South.

I had not heard that any of the other seminary students
who planned to be part of the SIM wanted to go to Ebenezer. Perhaps the name of Dr. King frightened them away. Or
perhaps it was my hand, waving with such frenzied intensity,
that discouraged others from competing with me for my first
choice. In any case, suddenly my name was written beside
Ebenezer on the blackboard, and the meeting quietly moved
on. Inside, I was terrified. My life was about to change in ways
I could never have anticipated.

As the news of my going to Ebenezer began to spread
around Union Seminary, where I was in my middle year of
study, many students and faculty didn't know what to make
of it. They said things like "Are you sure?" "Do you know what
you are getting into?" "Is this what you really want to do?"
and "I wouldn't, if I were you." I was beginning to be filled
with doubts, generated by the violence that had accompanied
Dr. King in the Montgomery bus boycott and the violence and
threats of violence surrounding the sit-in movement, which

at that time was generating momentum in the South. People were being beaten up, death threats were in the air, and the Ku Klux Klan seemed to be ominously growing in strength.

I had been drawn into the church by a gospel that sought to change the world for the better, and I was attracted to Ebenezer by Dr. King's compelling vision of freedom. Here was a Christian I wanted to follow and when the opportunity arose, I wanted to get as near as I could to this man of vision and action. Even though I was an Episcopalian, I knew I would learn a lot by working in a Baptist church that was alive with the social gospel. The threats of danger that seemed to me to be magnified by my wary friends began to worry me, I admit, but they also challenged me to go where few others had gone. I wanted to experience a church and a movement where social change engaged people's hearts and minds, and the possibility of becoming enveloped in the spirit of social transformation called me to take the risk. While I really had no idea what I was getting into and while I could read concern in the facial expressions of many people, a few rejoiced with me, and I leaned on their support.

A few days later, I went to my mother's for dinner. I had not told her of my plans, and I wondered what she would say. "Mom," I said, when we were relaxing before dinner, "I want to tell you of my plans for this summer." I could see that she was eager to hear, so I said, "I am going to work with Martin Luther King and be his assistant at the Ebenezer Baptist Church."

Her eyes opened, her mouth dropped. I suddenly feared her disapproval, and in the gaping silence I wished I hadn't said it. But all at once a great smile of joy and amazement spread across her whole face. "I am thrilled," she said. "Tell me more."

My mother had been a pioneer in her own day, although that was a long time ago. She had gone to medical school in 1923 and had spent the summer of 1926 in the Kentucky mountains, a medical student, taking medicine to a remote place that had never seen a doctor. I suddenly sensed that I was tapping into her pioneering, perhaps rebellious spirit and that I was following a path she had charted for herself some forty years before. A short while after our dinner together a friend told her with disapproving scorn, "He will never be a bishop if he works with Martin Luther King." My mother rose to my defense. She told him that having this experience was an extraordinary opportunity in my life and was not to be passed by. I treasured her encouragement.

Early one June morning, I started up my 1946 Chevrolet and headed south into a world I had never experienced and couldn't imagine. I left from Peninsula, Ohio, where I had been visiting Martha, my girlfriend. She supported me in the venture, and her words "Go for it" rang in my ears. I carried them with me all summer. "I can't wait to hear all about it. Write me every day," she said, and as I was climbing into my car she whispered, "I love you." I would marry her two years later, but now her whisper was like wind in my sails.

Beside me on the seat were my sleeping bag and some maps, as I was prepared to sleep out in the open air if the weather was good. For the first night, I found a beautiful secluded place overlooking a lake created by the Tennessee Valley Authority. The stars were bright overhead and the bugs were few. I awoke as the sun flooded the lake, turning the wisps of fog that drifted slowly with the wind into golden puffballs. I drove through the Great Smoky Mountains National Park, where I found a stream that was cold, fast, and clear. It served well as a place in which to shave and bathe. By this time the sun had warmed the rocks, and I rested there an hour or so, absorbed in the extraordinary beauty of the place and reflecting on the experience into which I was heading.

The farthest south I had ever been was on a vacation trip to Williamsburg with my family when I was about twelve years old. I had never lived in a black community or worshiped in a black church. I was full of excitement, but apprehension began to dominate my feelings as I drove deeper into this foreign land. All the questions with which I had been flooded before I left now clamored for answers. Why was I doing this? As an Episcopalian from the North, didn't I belong in the North? Was I going to be hurt? Would I be killed? Would I be rejected by the people I was going to work with? In spite of my fears, I kept my Chevy pointing south. The roads were endlessly long, and the early summer days already hinted at the terrible heat that was soon to come.

I was heading toward Ashville to a small conference organized for the white seminary students who would be working in black churches for the summer. When thunderclouds darkened the sky that evening, I found an inexpensive hotel for the night. The next day I joined about ten others at the conference. The most important part of that conference, which was to prepare us for the work ahead, was that I received $300 in cash. I was too shy to tell people that I had very little money and that even an inexpensive hotel was a serious strain on my wallet. "Oh, you're the one going to Ebenezer," several people commented. Yes, I acknowledged, recognizing that others felt this assignment was something special.

When I arrived in Atlanta on a Wednesday afternoon, I realized that I had no idea how I was going to find Ebenezer. Having no directions to the church itself, I headed into the heart of the city and drove around and around until I stumbled upon Auburn Avenue. As I began to drive down the street, I suddenly realized that everyone on Auburn Avenue was black, and I felt eyes looking at me from all directions, asking the hard question, What are you doing here?

I had to drive very slowly so I could read numbers, which attracted even more attention, but I kept going, saying to myself, "This is where I belong. Yes, Brewster gets Ebenezer. This is my home for the summer." All at once I found myself in front of the church. I parked, straightened my tie, and then, closing the car door behind me, I walked up the steps into Ebenezer Baptist Church.

2

Baptized with Fire

EBENEZER BAPTIST CHURCH looked huge to me. The large red brick sanctuary facing Auburn Avenue seemed solid as a rock, and I felt very small as I approached. To its left was a square building that contained rooms for meetings, classes, and offices. Opening the door, I saw that the vestibule led into a room where two secretaries worked. As I walked in, the crisp clicking of the two typewriters suddenly stopped. The three of us looked at one another, back and forth, until I broke the silence. "Hello. I'm Gurdon Brewster."

"Reverend Brewster," said the older of the two. "I'm Lillian Watkins, and this is Sarah Reed. We were expecting you."

After some introductions, Lillian said she would take me to Daddy King. Lillian was a large woman, warm and friendly, with a great booming laugh. I felt at home in her presence immediately, and I sensed we would have a good time together. We climbed the stairs and proceeded down the hall until we came to the door that said "Rev. M. L. King." She knocked and we walked in, and all at once Daddy King Sr. and I were shaking hands and greeting each other with vigor. He stood about five feet eight or nine inches tall, was large framed and solid. He had a big voice, a warm smile, and a robust laugh that carried a great distance. Born in 1899, he was full of life and energy, and immediately I was aware of the power of his presence.

I could sense that as they greeted me and genially asked about my long trip to Atlanta from the North, Lillian and Daddy King were looking me over carefully, up and down and through my eyes and into as much of my heart as they could see. I didn't realize it at the time, but I was the first white person to come as a worker in the church, and I am sure they were filled with as much apprehension and curiosity as I was. Having me there was a huge risk for them. Would I be regarded as an outside agitator, a white northerner intruding into an intricately balanced system? Would the church be threatened with bombs or with fire and would someone get hurt because of me? It was hard to assess the risks, but the risks were real. But at the time, I didn't think of the risks as much from their perspective as from mine — it was a huge risk for me.

"Brewster," Daddy King said, all three of us still standing, "we have a small problem." Right from the first meeting, he always called me "Brewster."

"Brewster, the problem is where you are going to stay. I wanted you to stay in the home of one of my parishioners, but last Sunday, after I announced this plan in church, nobody stepped forward. So for the first few days you will stay with me." After talking for a few minutes, he suggested that he show me his house and introduce me to his wife.

Out in the parking lot, he said, "Just follow me." I got his phone number, in case we got separated as we wound our way through downtown Atlanta during rush hour. Soon, however, our two cars, still together, came out into an area with attractive suburban houses, and I followed along until we found Dale Creek Drive.

"Bunch," he said, introducing his wife, "I want you to meet Brewster. Reverend Brewster." Mrs. King's real name was Alberta, but Daddy King always called her Bunch. She was the daughter of Reverend A. D. Williams, who had been the pastor of Ebenezer from 1891 to 1931. Reverend Williams, a leader in the black community during his pastorate, had built up Ebenezer to be one of the most influential churches in the South. Mrs. King had grown up in Ebenezer and had frequently played the organ and piano for the congregation. She was extremely warm, full of spirit and energy, and over the summer she looked after me with special attention. They led me into their split-level house and took me up a small flight of stairs to a room at the end of the hall, on the right. It was a comfortable room with windows that faced their street and the driveway. A fluffy towel was placed neatly next to the pillow. I unpacked, and soon the three of us were eating dinner together.

"We have to be back in church in an hour," Daddy King said, "so we must move right along. We are going to the Wednesday night prayer service at seven. I want you to come to that."

My excitement overcame my temptation to say that I was too exhausted to go to a prayer service after an extremely long day's drive, so I soon found myself walking into the regular Wednesday service. Someone was playing the piano and a group of about thirty people was singing a hymn. People kept entering until there were seventy-five to a hundred people present. Quickly looking around, I noticed that I was the only white person in the room.

This was my first introduction to black Baptist singing. Their hymns were not familiar to me, and the way they sang them was totally new. They sang slowly and with such power and feeling that I was swept up in the experience. After prayers, readings, and more hymns, Daddy King stood up and introduced me. "After the next hymn," he said, "Reverend Brewster will preach to us."

I sat down, stunned. After the hymn, I was to preach! I had never preached a sermon in my life. I was a hesitant public speaker at best, always nervous and always needing a full manuscript from which to read. I was thrown into a panic. One thing I knew was that I couldn't refuse. I couldn't stand up after the last stanza and tell them I had nothing to say. Somehow, that was unthinkable. I had to do something. I quickly decided I would speak on the beatitudes — because that was the longest passage I could think of. I could make my way one by one over the verses where Jesus blessed and pronounced woes on a large variety of astounding themes.

As people began to sing, Reverend King handed me a Bible. Fanning through the pages, I suddenly became aware that I didn't know where the beatitudes were. As the hymn pro-gressed, I searched desperately. Were they in Matthew, Mark, Luke, or John? By sheer good luck, or with the miraculous grace of God, as the congregation sang the hymn's final words, my eyes fell on the passage. As the congregation sat down I moved to the front and began to read.

"Blessed are the poor . . . "

When I finished the passage, I let the Bible fall to my side with my finger firmly planted in Luke, chapter 6, and said quietly, "Blessed are the poor." All of a sudden, a small man sitting just in front of me, not eight feet away, called out, "Yes, brother, preach to me!"

I jumped. This was immediately followed by another, who said, "Amen, brother," and soon a chorus of "Amen," "Yes, Lord," and "Preach to me" filled the room, before I had said anything.

Did I blush? Did I show my astonishment? Was my terror visible to everyone? This was not how preachers were greeted in the Episcopal churches I attended in New York.

I said a few words and then moved on to the next verses. Blessed are the hungry, and then blessed are the sorrowful, and each time I spoke, my faltering words and stumbling silences were met with responses that seemed to thunder around the room and penetrate my being like lightning bolts hurled at me one at a time to encourage me, to heat me up, and to make the holy passion come alive in the room. How could I respond? Somewhere in the middle of Jesus' curses — Woe to the rich, and the others that followed — I began to accept the responses, and I could see that I might even welcome them with a little experience.

I don't recall what I said that evening, and likely that is just as well, because that first sermon would probably rank as one of the worst the Christian church has ever had to suffer through. I finally sat down, and all I could hear was the slowly softening chorus of "Amen, brother," "Thank you, Jesus," "Yes, Lord." A few hymns and more prayers followed, and then the quiet humming of another hymn, slowly, reverently, as individuals whispered prayers about the concerns they carried, to be hidden within the quiet humming of the people and then gathered up with the others to be lifted to the heavens.

Then it was over. People swarmed around me and shook my hand: Mother Clayton, Deacon Edwards, Deacon English, Deacon Reese, Mrs. Berrien, and Mr. Grimes.

"How'd you like your first service?" Reverend King asked me as we drove home.

"Just fine," I said. "Oh, I loved it." But I never told him that it was the first sermon I had ever preached in my life.

3

Beyond Books

T HE FIRST THING I wanted to do was to meet the EYO,
the Ebenezer Youth Organization, with whom I would
be working, and have them show me downtown Atlanta. It
was already getting hot when we met on a Saturday morning
inside the church. Ronald, Laura, Godfrey, Denise, Beth, and
Jack, all high school students, joined me for the excursion.
Perhaps they were typical for a high school group because they
enjoyed many kinds of excitement, from taking trips, to having
parties, to reflecting deeply on the issues they were facing
in their lives. Intelligent and thoughtful, they became very
involved in my work during the summer and looked forward
to their teaching me about their lives and showing me many
things. Over the coming weeks these six, with several others,
would become the core of the group I would work with, and
they would introduce me to a world I had never known or
experienced.

Making our way on foot along Auburn Avenue toward the
center of town, they pointed out places where members of the
congregation lived and worked. I met Grimes, the custodian
of the church, who lived with his wife and twelve children
across the street from Ebenezer. Grimes, as everyone called
him, had spent time in jail, and Daddy King, believing that he
had been convicted unjustly, somehow got him released and
then gave him the job in the church, where he had served
for a number of years. When we walked into his yard, the

children poured out the door like ants when a stick is poked into their nest. Suddenly I was surrounded by the bold and the shy; they shook my hand amid the giggles and twitters of the youngest, who peeped at me from behind the frame of the door. Thereafter, I would always go out of my way to greet Grimes and his family as I went back and forth to the church.

Diagonally across from the church was a gas station owned by Jack's father, whom everyone called Smitty. We walked across the street and I was introduced to Mr. Smith. During our conversation I glanced over at his car, where I saw a bundle of fishing rods protruding from the trunk, with assorted floats, hooks, and dried-up worms hanging down in loose tangles. When I commented on these, he said he loved to fish, and when I told him that I was a fisherman as well, we had a good talk about fishing around Atlanta. "Hope you will join me some day," he said, and I tucked that into the back of my mind as something I would greatly enjoy. "Yes, I will," I told him. "I'll look forward to that."

We walked past the building where Dr. King Jr. had his second office, in addition to the office he used in Ebenezer. This was the headquarters of SCLC, the Southern Christian Leadership Conference, which had been created several years before. Walking a few blocks beyond that, we found ourselves in the center of downtown Atlanta.

The day had started hot, and I knew before long it would be a real sizzler. As our little group proceeded down Auburn Avenue in the midday sun, the heat became nearly overwhelming. We were full of cheer and I was full of curiosity, both to see the city for myself and to see it through the eyes of my companions, so there was never any hint of turning back. Before long we came to the largest store in Atlanta, Rich's Department Store. Pausing for a moment in a thin sliver of shade beside the building, we looked at the display windows and watched the people going in and out. I could see a lunch counter through the crowd and the thought of a cold drink suddenly became an obsession.

"Come on," I said. "I will treat everyone to a large, cold drink." I walked eagerly toward a newly vacated group of seats that curled around the lunch counter. I was very thirsty after walking the distance of Auburn Avenue in the sweltering heat, and I hurried inside. All at once, I realized I was alone. Turning around, I saw the group of six standing at the entrance. They hadn't moved.

I beckoned for them to come in, to sit next to me in the seats I was now saving, before they filled up. But they didn't come. I beckoned with my whole arm, but now I could see a strange expression on their faces. I realized that they saw me clearly but still they would not move. They remained huddled close together, looking at me. I slipped off my seat and went back to where they stood.

"What's the matter?" I asked.

Laura answered in a whisper, as the shadow of embarrassment swallowed up her face, "We can't go in there. We can't sit with you at the lunch counter."

I had heard about the segregation of lunch counters and I had read about segregation in the South and the recent sit-ins, but all the lectures and books I had devoured in preparation for this summer did not prepare me for this conversation. Here we were, in temperature hovering near one hundred degrees, hot, tired, and very, very thirsty from our long walk, with about eight seats at the lunch counter vacant, just a few feet away from us, and we couldn't sit in them to buy a cold drink and rest our feet. A flush of outrage came over me, but sizing up the situation immediately, I said, "Okay. I'll go in and get drinks for us and bring them out here." I took their orders and went to the counter.

I was still stunned and filled with anger. These young white waitresses who gladly served me would not have served one of my new friends. I soon received my order and brought the drinks out to the group, but I hardly knew what to say. Suddenly I realized that there was a wall that existed between us, and I felt terrible. I was embarrassed. As we sipped our drinks, they talked about lunch counters and discrimination, and how even the largest downtown department store in Atlanta would take all the money they wanted to spend on clothes and other items but would not let them sit at the lunch counter to sip a drink, cool down, and take a rest.

I had known of the four black students from Greensboro, North Carolina, who, on February 1, 1960, went to the Woolworth's lunch counter and gave their order. When they were refused service, they simply decided to stay, declaring that they would occupy the seats until they were served. Word of this spread quickly, and the next day more than two dozen students sat at the lunch counter, refusing to yield their seats to white customers who would have been quickly and courteously served. They brought their schoolbooks and turned the lunch counter into their desks. In spite of being heckled and threatened, they never left their seats. Within one week all the lunch counters in Greensboro were occupied. After that, the sit-ins spread over the state and into the neighboring states, all led by students. The sit-in movement had begun.

I hadn't realized that Atlanta was in the middle of intense negotiations. The downtown merchants, led by Mr. Rich, maintained their right to serve white people only. The students, together with black leaders and other supporters, mounted pressure to integrate all facilities. Black college students in Atlanta wanted to intensify the pressure through massive sit-ins, whereas college presidents, clergy, and other black leaders urged a process of integration through negotiation. Negotiations, however, were slow moving, and the racial pressure was mounting in the city during the weeks of that hot summer.

As we sipped our drinks in the shade outside the main entrance of Rich's, I began to read a wide variety of threatening expressions in the eyes of the people around us. The youth group looked like a beautiful group of kids to me, but I began to sense that people were wondering whether they were a mob with more sinister intentions. There were expressions and body language I hadn't yet learned to read, but I began to sense discomfort among my group and I suggested that we leave and continue walking around downtown Atlanta.

The drinks were large, and as we proceeded through downtown Atlanta, it wasn't long before the drinks wound their way through our bodies. As we passed Rich's again, we all admitted that we wanted to find a restroom.

"Let's go in here," I said, as we stood at Rich's main door watching customers go in and out. I immediately noticed a strange look coming over their faces, and for a split second they looked at each other.

"We'll see you in a little while, right here," they said, and they pointed to a sign above the door, in large black letters: "Men. For Whites Only."

I had never seen such a sign before. I stopped and gazed at it. I had read books and had seen photographs of many such signs, but to actually be separated from my friends by the directions on this sign was another thing entirely. I glanced over to my youth group and saw them disappearing through doors in the back of the store. "Colored People Only," their sign said.

I could feel my anger rising up again over this indignity. "This is what it's all about," I said to myself. This is the source of the outrage, smoldering among the roots of America.

A short time later we gathered again and meandered back up Auburn Avenue. I was embarrassed at what my people were doing to hurt Laura, Ronald, Godfrey, and the others in the group. How could this be happening in 1961? I had never seen anything like this in New York. Soon we were back at Ebenezer saying our farewells, and then I was alone in my Chevy heading back to my room in Reverend King's house.

I was shaken. This experience would change my life. Other experiences of the summer that followed would build upon it, but this day was the first time I had come face-to-face with such blatant discrimination. I began to wonder how, confronted daily with this indignity, I could ever be expected to contain my anger. For the first time in my life, I knew I had enough violence in me to tear the world apart. My blood boiled over and I could feel in my bones the will to destroy anything and anyone who would hurt my newfound friends, these brave and beautiful members of my youth group. I wondered if I ever could find enough compassion so that I would not be consumed with anger and hatred. I wondered how love could fit into this mixture of outrage, frustration, and sadness. And I wondered whether I was up to the struggles that might lie ahead.

4

My First Sunday

I WAS LOOKING FORWARD to my first Sunday at Ebenezer. I dressed slowly and carefully, checking out my Sunday clothes. Before leaving New York City I had bought a light gray suit at a used clothing store near 116th Street and Broadway. In the store, it had seemed like a fine bargain for $4.25, but as I put it on, I saw that it looked a little shabby. The creases weren't crisp and the jacket hung awkwardly. I now wished I hadn't been quite so cheap. It was Sunday, however, and that was all I had. My black shoes dated from much earlier days, when I had worn them for dancing school. I had learned the fox-trot and the Charleston in them, some eight years earlier.

Daddy King and I arrived at the church in separate cars. After introducing me to several people, he asked Mrs. Berrien, a parishioner and mother of Godfrey, a boy in my youth group, and Mr. and Mrs. English, parents of Ronald and Laura, also members of my youth group, to show me around while he went to a meeting with the deacons. The church was a swarm of activity before the service, and as we walked through the halls I could see classes of various sizes studying the Bible or making plans for upcoming events. Children were walking and running here and there, and as they saw me they came to an abrupt stop. I grabbed their hands in a happy handshake and greeting, and after that I always seemed to have a group of little children around me, grabbing my legs. I could hear the choir working through its morning anthems for the service.

A few minutes before the service, I joined Daddy King in his office to try on a black robe. I found one that fit me fairly well and soon we were walking through the narrow passage that brought the clergy onto the stage. As Dr. King was away, Daddy King and I shared the stage, sitting on opposite sides of the pulpit. The choir was singing hymns behind us, and the congregation was singing along with them. I began to sense that all eyes were focused on me.

Soon Daddy King stood up and the first hymn began. Seated between the choir and the congregation, I felt bathed in the powerful singing. As the last line of the hymn was sung, Daddy King went to the pulpit and announced, "Reverend Brewster will now say the pastoral prayer." I was thrown into a panic. He adjusted the microphone and then stepped back. Now all eyes definitely were on me. I rose, and as I slowly approached the pulpit I wondered if I would even have a voice, let alone words to speak.

In the religious services that I had attended, people very rarely stood up and said spontaneous prayers. Being an Episcopalian, I followed the Book of Common Prayer, most of which had been written several centuries before and had been distilled over the years into beautiful sacred poetry. By the standards of the Prayer Book, spontaneous prayers in the middle of the liturgy would certainly have seemed out of place. I had gone to a Quaker college and then to Union Theological Seminary, an interdenominational seminary with Presbyterian roots, and spontaneous prayer was not central to these traditions, either. When I was called upon to lead services at seminary, for example, I would have prepared carefully, writing down my words in full and only after much thought, with the application of what craftsmanship I could muster. But this Baptist tradition was guided by a theology that was new to me, which left ample room for the Spirit to come spontaneously alive in the present. The written word was often seen as an obstacle to the leader's spontaneous response to the Spirit.

But rising to the demands of spontaneous speaking was not my strength. My knees shook, and having had no warning that I would be asked to pray, I panicked. All at once, however, I was guided to a little word that I learned in a course I had taken from George Buttrick the semester before: ACTS. This word saved the day for me.

The letters of the word ACTS stood for adoration, confession, thanksgiving, and supplication. This is the backbone of one form of prayer, and on these bones I hung the countless prayers that I would end up giving that summer, beginning with this first one. I began with the adoration of God and then focused on the goodness of creation. After that, I moved to the confession, in which I focused on those things that might have gone wrong in our lives. Then I turned to the thanksgiving, in which gratitude was elevated over hardships and suffering, and I ended with supplication, in which I mentioned our wants and needs and those of the world. How relieved I was when I could finally sit down.

Soon Daddy King stood up to preach. I was filled with anticipation; I had looked forward to hearing him for a long time. He began slowly and quietly, but soon the volume of his voice and the power of his body seemed to take over the whole sanctuary. I had never seen anything like it. He pounded on the pulpit with such fierceness that I thought the wood might split. He pointed at people and called them by name. He questioned God. He stamped his feet. He trembled so violently that the platform shook. And all the while his words rang out with fervent intensity.

The congregation slowly began to come to life as people called to him to preach and then responded with "Praise God," "Yes, Lord," "Hallelujah," and many other vibrant phrases. As Reverend King moved toward his crescendo the congregation began to shout and clap their hands. Soon most of the people were on their feet. The emotional level was incredible. I almost laughed aloud to relieve my tension. After sustaining this for a few moments his words slowly became softer and he brought the people back into quiet meditation. Soon the choir began to sing, intuitively sensing the timing for their cue, and the congregation began to hum and sing along with them. This singing was followed by an altar call, in which Reverend King invited people to join the church. And then came the announcements. Reverend King introduced me, and now that people had had a chance to look me over, he asked if there was any family who would like to put me up for the summer. "Please speak to me after the service," he urged.

When the service was over, the congregation went to a large room downstairs for refreshments. Far across the room I noticed one white person. Without intending to, I kept this person in the corner of my eye as I was surrounded by people who wanted to meet me. The youth group gathered, and we planned our first meeting together. It felt good to be surrounded by Ronald, Jack, Laura, Godfrey, and the others I had seen the day before.

Gradually I began to follow the pull of the mysterious magnet toward this other white person in the room. Over the course of meeting and greeting people, we slowly drew closer together. Finally, next to each other, we warmly introduced ourselves. Esther Turner was a member of this church. She was a woman in her fifties, I would say. Over the summer she was to become a friend and a great support to me.

The experience of meeting her in that fellowship hour taught me something I would long remember about the bonding of races. Inevitably, Esther and I were drawn to each other because we were the only white people in the room. In later years, when black people gathered in the university dining room and in their own clubs and fraternities, I recalled

Esther Turner coming toward me in that church's gathering. When, in the name of integration, white people wanted to break up black enclaves and met strong resistance from the black people, I would sympathize with the blacks and stand up for their cause. When I asked white administrative officials who were advocating forced integration if they had ever been in a minority within a large group of people, inevitably they would say they hadn't. "If you had," I would say, "you would know what pulls them together. Something deep is happening. Don't break it up."

After supper we went to the Sunday evening service which was to begin at seven o'clock. There were always two services on Sunday, with the evening service following the same format, but lasting a shorter time and with fewer in attendance. There was the wonderful hymn singing, which was followed by the pastoral prayer "led by Reverend Brewster," a sermon by Daddy King, and finally more singing. Daddy King's evening sermon was not as long or as intense as his morning sermon, but I marveled at how this man could give two remarkable sermons on the same day. I had been with him nearly the whole day, and I had not seen him prepare this sermon. In his preaching he developed a biblical text and told stories and anecdotes that kept everyone completely enthralled. He was a supreme actor on stage, and the members of the congregation became engrossed participants in a wonderful drama. Preaching and the quoting of scripture flowed so naturally for him that I was amazed. In contrast I felt woefully inept. I stumbled in my prayers, and I became very self-conscious of this because I seemed to be praying all the time; at each Sunday service and several during the week, and at every meeting I attended, every birthday to which I was invited, and, in fact, just about at every occasion where I was present. I knew my prayers were a rigid stringing together of lifeless words, because I was far more concerned with my technique than with the possibility that the Spirit might find a crack in my phrasing that would enable it to breathe new life into the room. It finally took Annette, a very sick young girl from my youth group, whom I would meet in a few weeks, to teach me how to pray.

After we got home, I asked Daddy King if any family had come up to him to volunteer to put me up for the summer. "No" he said. "You will just have to stay with me for a few more days."

5

Breakfast

N̶O FAMILY came forward to take me in after my first Sunday. After several public announcements, behind-the-scenes phone calls during the week, and a second Sunday went by, still no one volunteered to house me for the summer. During this time, I stayed with Daddy and Mrs. King. I was very happy there, but I remained prepared to move at short notice. The days went by and then another Sunday and another, and no one ever came forward to take me in. Consequently, we adjusted to the likelihood that I would be staying with the King family for the duration of the summer.

I began to fit into a routine. The family had a dog named Tappy, and it soon evolved into a convenience for everyone that I would let Tappy out in the morning when I got up and let him out in the evening when I returned. Tappy was a little brown-and-white dog a foot or so high, with a happy face and a briskly wagging tail. When I let him out into the fenced-in yard, he rushed back and forth chasing away the squirrels that had taken over the place when he was confined inside the house. When he had driven them away to his satisfaction, he would go about his business and then return inside, filled with affection and showing off a grand sense of accomplishment. Tappy loved everyone, but he clearly loved Daddy King the most.

Mrs. King would soon appear in her dark blue bathrobe and floppy slippers and start cooking breakfast. She would typically serve grits, eggs, sausage or bacon, coffee, toast, and orange juice. Daddy King had an appetite for a good breakfast, and in those first days the three of us would gather around the kitchen table and chat about this or that while we devoured the large meal.

Grits were not new to me. My father used to make a dish of kidney stew and hominy grits, with generous pieces of bacon on the side, which we loved. He died when I was fourteen, and hominy grits and kidney stew seldom appeared after that. In Daddy King's house, grits were a staple, built up on each plate like a round volcano, with a large pat of butter carefully placed in the crater.

After I had been staying with them about a week, Mrs. King came down with the flu and was forced to stay in bed. I could hear them talking one morning as Daddy King got dressed. Suddenly the door opened a crack and Mrs. King called out, "Brewster, see what you can find for your own breakfast. I'm not coming down this morning." I felt audacious rummaging around in her refrigerator, but I found some eggs and the makings of a breakfast. Soon Daddy King appeared.

"You know, Reverend King," I said. "I'm a pretty good cook. I can make breakfast this morning."

"Are you sure?" he asked quizzically. "All right then, Brewster, I'll see what you can do."

After I showed confidence around the kitchen, he pointed out where Mrs. King kept everything. Soon the coffee was percolating, the bacon was sizzling, and the grits were gently bubbling on the back burner. "You're more than a pretty good cook," Daddy King admitted when the two of us finally sat down together to eat.

Mrs. King didn't get well for a number of days, and I gradually became the regular breakfast cook. Perhaps she began to enjoy staying in bed a little longer; I never knew. But from that morning on, I cooked breakfast for Daddy King and myself. I mastered the cooking of fine grits, and I managed to produce one notable breakfast after another, much to Daddy King's pleasure and Mrs. King's relief.

Naturally an early riser, I would get up and let Tappy out and start the breakfast cooking slowly. I have always loved breakfast smells, so I would start the coffee and put the bacon on low heat just to bring the smell into the house. I would then take a cup of coffee and ease into a comfortable chair in the living room, beside the sliding doors that looked into the yard. With a book or some other reading material, I would spend a few quiet moments before the rush of the day began. "Sure smells fine," Daddy King would often say as he descended the stairs to join me in the kitchen.

"Reverend King," I said, when the two of us were eating our breakfast one morning, "where did you grow up?"

"That's a long story," he answered, and then he grew quiet. Not wanting to let the story simply lie there like an old possum playing dead, I pressed on a little more.

"I'd like to know where you were born."

He paused a little and then said, "I was born in Stockbridge, Georgia, a long time ago. My father was a sharecropper in those days. I grew up on the farm helping him out."

At that point we were interrupted by the telephone, and my questioning had to stop. We were soon off to our offices in Ebenezer. However, the fact that his father was a sharecropper and that Daddy King had grown up helping on the farm caught my imagination. I knew nothing about the real life of a sharecropper. How did he get from working the farm with his father to becoming senior pastor of Ebenezer Baptist Church? How did he come so far? I couldn't wait to pick up the thread of this great man's story over another breakfast alone with him.

6

My, Oh My!

I HAD BEEN GIVEN a little room off the far end of the secretaries' office for my workspace. Originally it was the
mimeograph room for the church, and there were several
bulky machines, along with stacks of paper and office supplies
piled, shelved, and spilling over all around the place. With
the help of Lillian and Sarah a desk was cleared, a machine
or two removed, paper and materials relocated, and within
a short time the little room was arranged so that I could be
comfortable in it.

I soon realized that although it was noisy, small, and had
no windows, it had the great advantage of being right next to
Lillian and Sarah's office, where just about everything inside
and outside the church was loudly discussed. Much of this talk
was in some way connected with a joke, so besides listening
to the current gossip of the day, I was entertained by their
stories and guffaws. Sometimes I couldn't refrain from joining
them, so I left my little cubicle and laughed and joked along
with them.

One day a man named Frank came by to talk about arrangements for something. It was a long talk, and it ranged
over a number of topics. When he left, the office was
quiet for a moment until Lillian commented that Frank was
not married, though the woman he had recently been seen
with was.

27

"My, oh my," Sarah said. I was amazed at how much they knew about this man. "My, oh my," she said, breaking the silence a few minutes later and hinting that she knew far more than she wanted to say within my hearing.

The office was arranged in such a way that there was a counter that separated Lillian and Sarah's desks from the space where people came in and talked. As people entered the area, I learned to read the nuances of Lillian's greetings and so learned a volume about an individual before he or she even began to talk.

A few days later I saw Lillian rise slowly from her chair and quietly move toward her side of the counter. The door into the office opened and in walked an elderly woman. I noticed instantly something I had not seen in the office before. Lillian approached her with great affection and respect, standing to talk, offering to hold the door, and conducting the conversation with extreme politeness.

Lillian introduced me. "Mother Clayton, this is Reverend Brewster." Mother Clayton, in her late seventies or early eighties, was tall and very thin. She wore glasses and carried a large, bulging black purse that swung on a thin strap from her shoulder. She stood as straight as a telephone pole, comporting herself with great dignity and speaking slowly with carefully chosen words. Her eyes twinkled, but they seemed also to penetrate right into me. One could not help speaking truth to her.

Her visit was short and businesslike. After she left, Lillian and Sarah were quiet for some time. I wondered who this remarkable woman was. "That was Mother Clayton," Lillian said, as if saying it with special emphasis would tell me all I needed to know. "Mother Clayton is the conscience of this church. When she speaks, everyone listens, even Rev. She doesn't speak much but, honey, she is not afraid to speak to Rev like no other person in the world speaks to Rev. She is always right and he knows it. She is the only one who can put Rev in his place." She began to laugh.

"My, oh my," Sarah said in the background, and chiming in, she added, "She's not afraid of anything. You watch her on some Sunday. If there is a problem in the church, the eyes of every woman focus on Mother Clayton's pocketbook during the collection. If she pulls out small change, all the women follow her. If she is generous, the women follow that, too. They know what is generous for Mother Clayton. You watch her on Sunday mornings. She sits right in front of you, off to your right. See what she does."

"Reverend King must respect her a lot," I added.

"Lordy, yes," Lillian replied. She paused a moment and then looked at me. "You know, honey," she said, "around here people all know him as Daddy King. You can call him what you want, but to us, he's Daddy King."

"Thank you," I said, glad for the tip. Up until that point, I hadn't been sure what to call him, as Daddy seemed a bit too familiar to me. "But if he's Daddy King to you, then that's fine with me." I always addressed him, however, as Reverend King.

The phone rang, and soon, as others came and went, the office came back to its normal level of noise, energy, and amusement. I, however, was fascinated by Mother Clayton and wished I could get to know her. Who was this person who carried the respect of the whole church on her slightly built and elderly frame?

Many people entered the office and left, doing small errands for the church, but there were always a few who hung around and didn't seem to ever want to leave. One man, clearly well known by both women, leaned his big frame on the counter and looked back and forth from one to the other. Neither Lillian nor Sarah looked up. He began talking and they kept typing without saying a word. Not seeming to get the message, he moved over to a corner chair and just sat there, not reading, not talking, not even fidgeting about. He just acted as if he belonged to the office décor.

"I must be going," he finally said, and got up and left the room, walking out the door and looking happy and proud, as if he had just accomplished something important. The silence was finally broken by Sarah's loud exclamation. "My, oh my."

I slowly walked out of my office to get a sense of the situation. "Oh, honey," said Lillian, "what we know about him would burn your ears." But they never did talk about him again and burn my ears, much to my regret.

About my third day in the office, Mrs. King Sr. came in to say hello. Both Lillian and Sarah stood up to greet her.

"I just stopped by to see how you were doing in here," she said to me after greeting the others. She came into my little office and looked around. "Very nice," she exclaimed, after noticing how we had transformed the cluttered mimeograph room into a comfortable space. "M. L. is finally back in town, and you'll meet him today," she said.

She didn't stay long, but I felt she was keeping a benevolent eye on me and, in a gentle way, informing Lillian and Sarah that my well-being was important to her. I could sense the respect and affection they held for her, and I greatly appreciated her visit.

Not long after she left, Dr. King walked into the office. While I had anticipated meeting him with much excitement, deep down I was filled with fear and awe. I cold not imagine how he had led the Montgomery bus boycott, described so well in his book *Stride toward Freedom*, through bomb threats to his family and through endless hate letters and calls. Living under the constant threat of death, he possessed courage that was beyond my comprehension. I wanted to be near this Vesuvius of courage, hoping that some of this fire would enkindle into flame my smoldering spirit.

His vision for a new America, and his method of bringing us there, so inspired me that I wanted to be immersed in this vision and practice as part of my life and education. The evils of racism and of poverty caused by economic and social exploitation were the great issues that white America refused to address. I could not sidestep them, however, and remain true to my inner convictions of faith any longer. While I knew that I wanted to be exposed to him, I was terrified at the same time. Would I have to change in ways that scared and threatened me at the core?

Here was a man who practiced nonviolent resistance to these evils through the practice of radical love. What an incredible vision. What would he expect of me? It was hard enough for me to love my friends and family members, but how could I love an enemy? I had spent my life living in such a way that I would have no enemies. This seemed to be the way of life for people who had been given many advantages. Would he see through me and find a hollow shell of a Christian? Would he find a coward ready to embrace a liberal idea but afraid to follow a liberating action? Would he think my presence was motivated more by a white person's guilt than by my genuine desire to be challenged? I wanted to make a positive contribution, but I admit I was afraid of what this might mean for me.

There was a flurry of greeting as both Lillian and Sarah rose to welcome him. Suddenly ducking nimbly under the swinging flap in the counter he extended his hand to me. "Reverend Brewster. It is so good to have you here. I have heard a lot about you. How are things getting on?"

He was not a large man, probably five foot seven or eight, with a very different build from his large-framed father. At thirty-two years old, he filled the room with his energy. After looking at my space and noting the temperature in the office, he asked me to join him on the front steps, where it was cooler. He asked me about my seminary studies and my trip to Atlanta, and he wondered if I was comfortable staying with his parents. "I hear you do some fine cooking," he said with a laugh. "My father says you make grits like a southerner." He laughed. We both realized the humor of the situation.

Our first conversation was short, and it was interrupted a number of times by people driving by and waving or stopping to chat. After I told him I looked forward to more talks, he said he was going to a training conference on nonviolent resistance in Alabama in a few weeks and he hoped I would be able to be there.

"Yes," I told him. "I will look forward to that."

"Have you ever had training in nonviolent resistance?" he asked me. I told him I hadn't. "I think you will learn something," he said. "This is the way we resist and change oppressive laws, through nonviolent resistance," he said, and paused. Then he added, "I hope you will have a good experience this summer. This is a good summer to be in Atlanta. There is a lot going on." With a strong handshake, he got up and left.

I watched him drive down Auburn Avenue. I felt excited to have met him, but I was also afraid of what I might have to go through during my training in nonviolence. I wondered if I would ever be called upon to put it to use. I had already had a very minor brush with segregation laws and I had felt many things, but nonviolence was not one of them. His comment "I think you will learn something," said in an offhand manner, went right to the core of my vulnerability. Would I be called upon to receive punches and kicks from a white racist and not be able to kick and punch back? Would I even put myself in that situation or would I hold back and let others take the heat?

"Walk the talk," they said in the movement. I could do plenty of talking, but my, oh my . . . I wondered if I could do the walking.

7

Surprised by Danger

ESTHER TURNER, the only white member of the congregation, invited me to spend Saturday afternoon with her and her husband, Bill, at their farm, so on the following Saturday I drove my Chevy along the roads leading out of Atlanta. About half an hour from the city I found the exit from the highway and the small road that finally led to their long driveway. They had a farm of about thirty acres, with rolling pastures and split-rail fences. Two dogs — a yellow lab and a golden retriever — romped freely about the place. Her son was a jockey and horse trainer, so although I saw no horses, I knew that horses were part of their life.

After a short tour around her place, Esther left Bill working on a project and came to join me. Sitting comfortably on their porch with cold lemonade to sip, we began the first of many long conversations about the work of the Kings, the civil rights movement, and my life that summer. Over the following weeks, I came to learn much from her about the movement and the people in the church.

Esther had become a member of Ebenezer more than a year before I arrived, responding to Reverend King's altar call one Sunday morning, after having given it much thought over preceding months. She had been involved in the civil rights movement for much of her life, and when her husband, Bill, moved to Atlanta, she became involved in the life of Ebenezer. A person of deep faith, she was wise and well informed, a perfect teacher for me at that time. "One morning during the sermon," she said, "it just felt like the right thing for me to do. I walked up the aisle and was warmly received by the people — the only white member of the congregation."

She asked me what I had been doing, and after filling in some details, I told her about my excursion down Auburn Avenue and into Rich's department store with some of the youth group. When I talked about what I found there and the reaction of the youths, she laughed and laughed. "What is so funny with that?" I asked.

"Did you know what you were walking into?" she exclaimed. I said I was learning, but at the time I didn't know much about the specifics of the movement in Atlanta.

"You almost walked right into a hornet's nest," she said. "Did you know that Dr. King had been arrested there? Can you imagine how many eyes were focused on you and your youth group? A few seconds after your arrival, your presence was probably known by Mayor Hartsfield." I asked her to tell me the story, because I wanted to learn more about what I, in my innocence, had almost walked into.

The previous October, she told me, Dr. King went into Rich's with a group of students to test whether they would be served at the lunch counter. He had been arrested along with the others, and that was when he spent his first night in jail. I had known that Dr. King had been arrested, but I hadn't realized he had been arrested in the very store where I had taken my youth group. That was just the beginning of an amazing story that she went on to describe.

He spent his first night in jail because he refused bail. "Jail no bail" was the slogan everyone chanted. Meanwhile, crowds gathered outside the jail, singing and chanting and waiting around nervously. Soon the mayor and the governor, as well as Daddy King and other black leaders, became involved. In the middle of the night, Dr. King was taken away in handcuffs and leg irons, placed in the back seat of a police car right next to a police dog, and driven to another jail. His wife, Coretta, became extremely upset when she heard where he was — in a Georgia country jail, where anything could happen. She was pregnant with her first child at the time and afraid for her husband's life.

Esther knew the details of the recent history, so I asked her to fill me in. Dr. King's arrest came toward the end of the presidential campaign between John F. Kennedy and Richard Nixon. Which one of the two would receive more of the black vote was of crucial importance in the election. Someone inside Kennedy's campaign committee persuaded Kennedy to call Mrs. King about her husband's arrest when Dr. King was in jail. They had a brief conversation at the end of which Kennedy offered his assistance. News of the phone call spread throughout the black community like an electric shock, and soon it had traveled all around the country. Dr. King, who had been sentenced to hard labor in a chain gang, was suddenly freed.

There was a rally right after his release at Ebenezer, which Esther attended. This rally, she believed, changed the course of American history. Reverend King was angry at the treatment his son had received, and when he got angry, everyone trembled. He began to speak and the room was tense. He spoke about the jail sentence and what it was like in jail, and then he began to talk about Kennedy's call to Coretta. There was a long pause. He said that if that man had the courage to call Coretta, "I have the courage to vote for him." At that point, he took off his Nixon button and put on a Kennedy button. "Roman Catholic or not, I'm voting for him."

Everyone was shocked. Esther could see Nixon buttons coming off lapels as Daddy King changed sides. Soon Dr. King came in and everyone stood and cheered. He was embarrassed, it seemed, over his father's sudden switch from Nixon to Kennedy, and he didn't immediately go along. He wanted to stay out of partisan politics. Dr. King told his story in an eloquent way, and without aligning himself with his father, he focused on his experience and how this should help mobilize protests in the future. "We must master the art of suffering. We must learn the art of creative suffering for a higher cause," he said.

She paused a moment. "Master the art of suffering for a higher cause," she slowly repeated. "This gets to the heart of struggle, doesn't it?" Yes, I thought, but what does that really mean? Did I know how to suffer for a higher cause? Does America know how to suffer for a higher cause? I had been aware of some of the broad dimensions of the Atlanta movement, but the deep spiritual life of the people involved was beginning to break through to me. Of course, I thought, how else could one sustain such commitment? And I had never heard the details from anyone who had been directly involved, so I asked her to continue.

"That meeting decided the election," she went on. "Negroes all over the country took off their Nixon buttons and put on Kennedy buttons. Those votes made the difference in that very close race. Some people said that the election was won because of that one phone call."

We began to talk of my summer plans and what I hoped to accomplish while I was in Atlanta. I valued Esther's opinion as I tested out my thoughts, which were slowly taking form. It seemed to both of us that it was important for me to spend as much time as possible getting to know the members of Ebenezer.

"Get to know the Kings and their families," she recommended. "And get to know the life of the parish."

We thought it also would be important for me to meet white clergy and white parishes. I shared with her my plan for a conference of youth groups from white and black churches to meet with Dr. King later in the summer. I would learn a lot from this, she thought. She encouraged me to get to know the people in the SCLC office and to find out what their programs were during the summer.

A car drove by, interrupting us with several loud honks. "What was that all about?" I asked.

"I suspect it is someone from the local KKK," she said, passing it off as if it were nothing.

"The Ku Klux Klan is out here?" I exclaimed.

"Oh, yes," she replied.

"Have you ever seen a burning cross?" I asked.

She laughed. "Oh, yes. I have had them burn on this place, out there by the road," she said, again almost as if it were a routine occurrence.

"Right out there?" To me, the KKK was a mysterious and terrifying organization, completely foreign to my experience, and I was amazed at how casually she spoke about it.

"They have rallies and cross burnings on the outskirts of town," she said.

"Do you know any member?" I asked.

"I am sure I do, but they never tell me, so I don't know whom I know or who among Bill's acquaintances might be a member. It's all very secret. But I know I'm not one of them."

The afternoon flew by, and after dinner I left for Atlanta. As I was leaving, she said, "You know, we could put you up here for the summer. But I think it would be better if you stayed with some family besides us."

"Yes," I agreed. "Thank you, anyway."

My car was low on gas, so I swung into a small gas station before the country road joined with the highway. "Fill it up, please," I said to the attendant.

Four men were leaning against an old pickup, casually passing the summer evening. I noticed them turn to look at me, one by one. At first I thought nothing of it, but then I realized that they all were staring at me while they leaned their backs against the rusty cab and fenders. After I paid my bill I needed to use the restroom, so I pulled my car nearer to the restroom and went in.

While I was in the restroom, the door suddenly opened and one of the men entered. He was about my age and height, but much heavier than I. He carried a beer can in one hand and a cigarette in the other. The cigarette pack was rolled up in his T-shirt sleeve and bulging on his shoulder.

"You a nigger lover?" he asked. I remained quiet but my heart was racing. "You a nigger lover from the North?" he asked again, this time demanding an answer. I realized they had seen my license plate on my car and heard my northern accent. All at once, I knew that I was alone and cornered in the restroom.

"No," I answered. "Just visiting an old friend." He nodded his head, pausing, as we both stood facing the urinal.

"That's good," he replied. "We have a way of keeping northern troublemakers from making any trouble," he said, making a sweeping gesture with his hand and splashing a spray of beer on the floor.

When I opened the door I was met by the stares of the other three men leaning against the front of the truck, which faced the restroom's entrance. "Hello," I said, trying to look confident and act pleasant as I headed toward my car.

"Visiting an old friend," the man said to the others, as he followed me out. They shifted positions as I walked near them, each clutching a can of beer and smoking a cigarette. I heard one man spit on the ground as I got into my car. They muttered something that I didn't hear as the door closed with a thud. Backing the car around, I eased my way onto the road and took off, checking the rearview mirror frequently to see if I was being followed.

Out on the highway heading toward Atlanta, it took a long time before my heart rate settled back to normal. I realized that I had been unthinking and careless to let myself get cornered in a bathroom in rural Georgia by a menacing group of white men who knew I was from the North. I had to put my sheltered ways behind me. I had nearly walked into another hornet's nest. Never again, I said to myself. I needed to learn how to hone my peripheral vision and my sixth sense to pick up danger signals before they erupted into violence. It was clear I had much to learn.

Driving along, still terrified at what had happened, I pictured myself getting into a fight, being hit on the head with a pipe, tossed into the back of the pickup, and dumped off in the woods far out of the way. I would have disappeared, and my Chevy would have turned up abandoned along some dirt road many miles away. Danger had caught me by surprise for the second time in a few short weeks. I was ashamed of myself. I realized that I had to get smart, real fast.

How differently things might have turned out if those men had actually known where I was about to spend the night!

8

Sherry and Smoke

THE NEXT SUNDAY AFTERNOON, while I was reading in the living room and Daddy King was taking a nap, the door swung open and Dr. King walked in. The day was hot, and after greeting me, he went to the refrigerator to find something cold to drink.

"How are things going?" he asked as he pulled up a chair nearby. After an easygoing exchange, I told him about my encounter in the gas station the day before. He listened with full attention as I told the story of being cornered in the restroom. "You don't want to do that again. You've got to be careful."

As he said this, Daddy King came in. He had heard some of my story, and he commented, "You've got to watch your step, Brewster. That's white trash. They'll kill you and drop you over the bridge into some black river out in the country, and no one will find you. Members of the KKK, I'm sure they were."

After some more talk, Dr. King asked me if I had developed any plans for the summer. I told him of my plan for a gathering of youth groups from white and black churches. "I'd like to pull groups together and have you come and talk with them. I thought I would try to be a bridge builder between the white and Negro youth groups. Maybe you could join us for a short time."

Both Daddy King and Dr. King agreed that that would be worth trying. "See if you can work it out. I'd be glad to help you if I'm in town," Dr. King said.

Soon Mrs. King Sr. appeared. I went up to my room because I felt in the way when Dr. King visited his parents.

The next day at the office I was highly motivated to start calling white churches, to see if I could meet with clergy and present my plan. The more I thought about this plan, the more excited I became. To have youth groups from black and white churches meet together and hear Dr. King talk about his experiences in the Montgomery bus boycott, and to listen to him spell out his vision for integrating America, seemed like a compelling theme for a day's conference. It was an event that I hoped would have a positive impact on the lives of the young people as well as on their churches.

Soon I was thumbing through the phone book looking up the numbers of Episcopal churches. I had decided to start with Episcopal churches because that was my denomination and the one I knew best. I decided to start at the top, so I called the diocesan office and asked if I could speak to someone involved in social ministries. I spoke to a secretary of one of the bishop's assistants who, in a lovely southern voice, got all the details of the purpose of my visit and set up an appointment for me. About an hour after hanging up, she called me back.

"You're working with Ebenezer Baptist Church, where Reverend King Sr. and Dr. King Jr. are co-pastors?" she asked, and after a few more questions she said she looked forward to seeing me. After she hung up, I wondered what that call was about. It felt strange to me, because I had told her all those details just a few moments before.

Nevertheless, I went back to the phone to continue my round of calls. I picked out four churches, and of these, I made appointments with two for later in the week. The other

churches seemed to have legitimate reasons for delaying meetings: at one, the rector was away; at the other, the youth group
was not meeting for the summer. My calendar now had some
specific dates written it, and I felt I was making progress. I
looked forward to the days ahead.

Several days later I walked into the diocesan office. I saw
that everyone else was impeccably dressed, and I suddenly
felt self-conscious in my four-dollar suit and my black shoes
from high school dancing classes. Two men who walked past
me were wearing crisp dark suits and clerical collars, and the
women sitting behind desks in their offices wore attractive,
expensive-looking dresses.

When I greeted the receptionist, she looked up and in a
thick southern drawl said yes, I did have an appointment on
the calendar, but unfortunately, the other party couldn't make
it. Surprised, I asked if I could schedule another appointment.
"I will give him the message and he will get back to you about
when he is free," she said.

As I turned to leave, I saw several men looking at me from
their offices and I wondered whether one of them was the
man I was supposed to see. I had a lot to say as well as a lot
to learn, but something told me that I was being brushed off.
He didn't want to see me. I had thought I could create an
important connection between the diocese and Dr. King and
the black community. What's going on here? I wondered.

Later that morning, I had an appointment at a suburban
church several miles outside the city. As I entered the large
parking lot, I noticed that my '47 Chevy was by far the oldest
among the several parked cars. I walked in and was greeted
warmly by a young priest who wore a well-pressed, light blue
suit over his black shirt and clerical collar. He ushered me
into his office, inviting me to sit in a comfortable, dark blue
chair. He looked at the clock and studied it at some length.

"I don't think it is too early for a little glass, do you?" he asked. "The sun is just about to pass over the yardarm." He laughed, giving a forced, wicked twist to his intonation.

"Sounds fine," I said, and after a quick glance around the room, I asked, "Where do you keep it?"

"Oh," he replied, showing more energy than he had before, as he jumped up from his chair and walked toward the bookcase shelf. Pulling out a large volume of Shakespeare and an oversize Bible, he reached into the dark cavity and pulled out his secret decanter of sherry and two glasses. Acting very pleased with himself, he poured out two glasses and sat down.

"Nice sherry," I commented.

"Very," he replied with satisfaction. Then he began to talk about his work in the parish. "I have been here for two years," he said. I listened patiently, slowly sipping my sherry. Finally, I felt that I had a break when he got up to refill our glasses.

"What are some of the hardest issues you face? Do you deal with racism in any way?" I asked him, trying to direct the conversation in a more challenging direction.

"The main issue," he said, "is worship. Our worship service — Oh," he interrupted his thought, "we have no Negroes in our congregation." At this I began to talk about my work for the summer and my plan for a gathering of youth groups with Dr. King.

"We've never done anything like that," he said. "I'd have to bring the issue to my boss and also to the parents. Would you like some more?" he asked, holding the decanter perilously high over my glass, which was still more than half full.

"Is there much concern about civil rights, Dr. King, or the lunch counter sit-ins?" I asked.

"Oh, you know. People talk about it, but we don't get involved." He got up, walked over to the window, and brought the conversation back around to his work, his seminary, his hopes for the future, and his sherry. It took effort to bring the conversation back to my issues. By now my head was beginning to spin. I nevertheless found another opening. I told him I thought we could learn something from listening to Dr. King and having our youth groups come together.

"We'll just have to think it over," he answered. I told him I would call him in about a week to see what he thought after talking with people in the church, but I was beginning to feel that his interest was far more focused on his sherry than on current events.

I walked out to my car after saying good-bye, thinking that he had drugged me with sherry. I had been unable to move our conversation in any significant direction. I was baffled. How could he not be excited by my idea? I drove out of the church driveway and parked some distance away to collect my thoughts, and then slowly continued on to my next appointment.

The next church was even larger, newly painted, and well kept. I still believed in my idea, so when I met the minister I was still filled with enthusiasm. He was a middle-aged, energetic man, and he brought me into his richly carpeted office, well appointed with fine old wood, leather, and books. As he sat down, he reached into his pocket and pulled out his pipe. He then embarked on an elaborate ritual of pipe cleaning. First he cleaned out the bowl with a special tool that, before he began, he tossed into the air and caught with a dexterity that revealed a practiced hand. He next took out a white pipe cleaner and worked the inside of the stem. I sat still, enveloped in the folds of an overstuffed armchair, and said nothing as I watched him perform with full concentration his pipe ritual.

"What can I do for you?" he finally asked in a most inviting voice, trying to show real interest in me. He listened attentively as I spoke, giving me ample time to describe what I was doing for the summer.

"I like this parish to be on top of issues," he commented. "We are a leader among the churches. I think people would say that, if you asked them. Let me hear more," he said. "Of course, you would need to have police around," he added, almost as a footnote.

"Police?" I asked. I had never thought of needing police.

"Just in case," he replied. "You know, just in case." I quickly thought of Laura, Ronald, Denise, Jack, Godfrey, and the others members of the youth group. This man thought he needed police to protect his youth group from them. I couldn't believe what I was hearing, but he continued, "I know their parents would need to know there were police around — just in case. Just to be on the safe side. And, of course, I would want to record the event. Just to be safe."

"Well, frankly, I hadn't thought that we needed police," I replied.

"Well, you know what I mean. Just in case. Just to be safe."

I realized that in spite of his desire for police protection, I had touched off more than a little spark of interest. He pictured himself as a liberal and as a man who liked to be out in front on social issues, so I thought he would support my idea. By this time the smoke in the room was thick and stifling. I began to feel as if I were being smoked out the way a beekeeper smokes out a colony of bees to disorient and pacify them. I pressed my point again, emphasizing the extraordinary opportunity this summer afforded the churches.

"Timing is all-important," he said. "The timing isn't quite right." I felt him suddenly backing off. "The Negroes are moving just a little too fast. Timing is all-important," he said again, with added emphasis.

When I heard the words "too fast," I knew exactly where he stood. That was the telltale phrase. What else was there to be said? Soon he stood up, signaling an abrupt end to our conversation.

"I'll be in touch in a week or so," I told him, and he thanked me in a most genial way for coming all the way out to see him.

Cloaked in an atmosphere of thick southern charm, I was graciously ushered out the door. With no rancor, with no wrinkles in the pressed linen of genial conversation, and with no hint of animosity, my idea for engaging others in this important issue of the day and inviting them to meet the man at the center of it all had generated absolutely no positive response. My enthusiasm had been completely brushed aside.

The three appointments, which could have led to the beginning of something important in Atlanta, evaporated into thin air. Three at bats and three strikeouts. Once I had said what my intentions were, it seemed as if they wanted me out of their offices as fast as possible.

At first I was simply surprised. Before my visits, I had thought that I would find some agreeable colleagues who would support me or who would at least be interested in what I was doing. I had not succeeded in eliciting even one good question from them about my work. I began to feel a flicker of anger welling up from deep inside. History was being made right before their eyes and the clergy and the churches could become involved if they chose to. But it seemed that they wanted no part of it.

For the first time, I began to wonder how I would fit into a church structure in the future if this was what I was going to find. Having finished my second year in seminary, and being only two years out of college, I began to question where I fit in for my life's work. Then my mind shifted to how I was going to tell my youth group and Dr. King that the white people I had met with didn't want to see them, didn't even want to meet them. I imagined that if I told this whole story of rejection, the question forming in the minds of the youth group would be, What is wrong with us? I was feeling very protective of them, and I didn't want anything I said or did to be another source of their rejection and pain.

I could still hear the man's spit splatting at my heels a few days before as I walked to my car at the gas station, and I could feel the empty smiles that coolly brushed me off in the diocesan office. Now, however, I could also hear the church doors shutting behind me with the crunch of solid brass and heavy wood, following some genial words of farewell. What were the real differences between them, I wondered? The answer was hidden somewhere in the swirling of sherry and smoke.

9

Pick Yourself Up, Brewster

MOST MORNINGS I followed the breakfast routine I had established during my first week in Atlanta. I got up before seven, knowing that Daddy King liked breakfast around eight. I'd have a few pieces of bacon crackling in the skillet by 7:30, sending the aroma through the house, because Daddy King said he liked that smell when he was getting up. I held some of it back until just before he came in, so it wouldn't be too crisp or dried up. I set the grits cooking on the back burner and the coffee percolating beside the bacon. I let Tappy out to drive the squirrels up the oak trees and let him back in again when he was sure the yard belonged to him alone. Then I had time for a little reading in the easy chair beside the picture window.

The morning after I visited the churches, Daddy King asked me how my week had gone. "What did you find?" he asked.

I told him the man in the diocesan office had stood me up and that I'd felt strange, as if all eyes were on me when I awkwardly asked about my appointment. Then I told him about the other two visits. The first minister talked only about himself and showed no interest in my plan to involve his youth group, whereas the second minister seemed fearful, suggesting that police protection might be needed. Daddy King shook his head and said nothing.

These three visits were all that I had turned up after many phone calls and much persuasion. I didn't tell him that the first man had plied me with sherry and that the second nearly smoked me out. I didn't tell him how little interest had been shown in talking about desegregation or civil rights. And I didn't want to tell him that they weren't even interested in meeting his son. The negative responses of the white churches deeply embarrassed me as a white man. I felt they were really rejecting Daddy King and Dr. King and everything they stood for.

I think Daddy King saw how discouraged I was. He sat there in silence, scraping up the last pieces of bacon and mixing them with his grits.

I decided to turn the conversation back to his life. "Reverend King, you said you grew up on a farm and your father was a sharecropper. I'd like to know about that." How did it happen, I wondered, that he wasn't a sharecropper on a white man's farm somewhere in rural Georgia?

"That was a long time ago," he said, his eyes beginning to look out on a long sweep of far-off history. His parents were sharecroppers, he told me, farming somebody else's land. He was the second of nine children, the oldest boy. It was not easy in those days to feed nine children plus his mother.

"I was raised on a dead-end road," he said, pausing to slowly repeat it for emphasis. "A dead-end road." His father and mother worked hard from daylight to dark and got little or nothing for it. His father wanted him to be a sharecrop farmer just as he was, but Reverend King hated farming as a boy, just as his father hated farming. Still, his father thought that what was good enough for him was good enough for his son. His father wanted him to be farming at his side all day so he could take over and eventually enable his father to ease off from the hard work as he got older. They grew vegetables and had a few chickens, and sometimes a mule and a cow.

"I know something about milking a cow," I said as I formed my hands and went through the motions of milking a cow. He began to laugh, and all at once his hands went up and down. For a moment we were laughing together uproariously, pretending to be milking cows.

"You look like you know how to get milk from a cow," he said. Then he went on, telling me how he hated that life. He was driven like his father's mule. If you got angry with the white folks, they would either kill you or drive you off the land. His father learned to hide his anger under his smile to keep alive.

"Were you ever driven from the land?" I asked. He paused for a long time, looking out into the yard as if it were the field of his boyhood, stretching out into the distance. "Oh, my. There was one time I remember . . . ," he said. "You want to hear about all this?" he asked.

"Yes," I said, eagerly. "Yes, I do."

He then told me that his father, whom, he called Papa, worked for a man everyone called Settle Up because he was the one you would settle up with during the year and at harvest time. One day Mike, as his father called him, rode the old wagon behind their mule and sat right up there with his father. They had a load of cotton. His father told him to say nothing, but Daddy King had a head for numbers. When Daddy King saw Settle Up cheating his father, he spoke up. He thought there would be a fight right then, as people standing around were just itching to see a fight. His father didn't back down the way Settle Up thought he should. Settle Up finally gave them the money he owed, but Daddy King's father beat him on the way home for speaking out.

That night he heard the noise of a mob of men. His father ran out into the woods behind the house carrying his gun with him, and Daddy King's mother went to the door. He said he never forgot what he saw that night — a mob of white men with guns.

"I want you niggers off my land by tomorrow night," Settle Up hollered, and then after pausing, he spat out, "Or else."

"That 'or else' came crashing down on me, and I knew what it meant," said Reverend King.

"What did you do?" I asked.

The next day, he said, they gathered all their possessions together and took off walking down the road with nowhere to go but down the road somewhere. They left behind the cow, the mule, the chickens, the garden full of vegetables they had planted, and everything they couldn't carry with them. They lived beside the woods for a few days, and finally someone gave them an old, leaky shack to live in. They didn't have much to eat. His father would bring in a rabbit once in a while, or a squirrel, and his mother would stretch it out into a stew for the whole family. His father took to the bottle and his mother ironed clothes for white folks which earned her a little money.

Daddy King spoke slowly, thinking back on those times, and I waited for him to continue. His father hated to run, he said, but he had to live, so running and hiding was what he did. That way of life took a heavy toll on his father. A Negro, he went on to say, was just a thing, just an object, not a person. Just nothing. He told me how he hated the look in his father's eye when he knew they were out to get him and he had to run away and hide.

"What's a man to do?" he mused. His father had just asked for what was rightfully coming to him. "I hate that look in a man's eyes when he's afraid, and in his head he's running away with no place to go and no place to lay his head."

"I don't see you running away from people," I said to him.

"No, Brewster, I guess I don't." he replied. "Once you start running away, I don't know how you ever stop. I couldn't see

myself running away all my life. I wanted something more."
He paused again, and we were quiet for a few moments.

I asked him about his mother, and when he spoke I could
hear in his voice his affection and respect for her. She wanted
him to have schooling, but his father wanted him to grow
crops on the farm just like his father had. She was a hard
worker, working the farm and doing everything else to keep
the family together. In months when his father was in the
woods and hiding, or off drunk somewhere, she did it all,
working odd jobs for some white folks and doing whatever
they didn't want to do for themselves.

"She did their hard work for them," he said thoughtfully.

She sent him to the local school they were allowed to attend, and she took him to revivals, where he could hear some
preaching. "There was some mighty fine preaching in those
days," he said, pausing again and shaking his head.

"Your mother must have been quite a woman," I said. In
the pause, I could see him rolling some story over in his head
and I wanted him to continue.

"You want to hear something about my mama?" he asked.
He began to tell me about one day when he was a young boy.
He was carrying things down the road for his mother — milk
from the cow, and butter. He came upon a group of men, and
Settle Up was there. They asked him to do some petty job for
them, and he told them he was on an errand for his mother.
Settle Up pushed him, and the milk and butter spilled on the
road. He tried to wriggle loose but his shirt tore, and when
Settle Up pushed him to the ground his face got bloody. He
went home with an empty pail and blood streaming down
his face.

"Good Lord," Daddy King said, filling up with anger, "my
mother went into a rage. She grabbed my wrist right here,"
he said, showing me his right wrist, "and dragged me down to
where Settle Up was standing with his men.

" 'Who done this?' she asked, looking at me. I pointed to Settle Up.

" 'Did you hurt my boy?' she asked, walking right up to him.

" 'What of it? That nigger boy needs to learn to listen to me.' "

Sitting on the edge of his chair, Daddy King described what happened next. "I've never seen anything like it," he said. His mother was strong. Her arms had done a lot of hoeing and hauling and a lot of scrubbing. She balled up her fist and hit Settle Up and drove him to the ground, pounding his face all over. The men just stood around looking. They knew she was right. Then she got up. "Don't you ever touch my boy again, do you hear?" she said. With that she grabbed his wrist and left.

"I can still hear Settle Up over all these years, just as clear as yesterday," Daddy King said. " 'If I see your nigger, I'll kill him,' Settle Up said."

His mother didn't look back; she just clamped her hand around his wrist like a vise and walked home. She walked without saying a word. When they got near home she said just one thing.

" 'Don't you ever tell your father about this. He will try to kill Settle Up, and he'll surely die. Now promise me.' I promised."

There was a long pause after this.

Finally, I broke the silence and asked, "How did you get to Ebenezer?"

He described his father walking behind a mule, going back and forth and making rows on another man's land, like he was caught in prison and couldn't escape. All Reverend King wanted to do was to escape for himself. He just waited for his time.

"So what did you do?" I asked. He described what it was like to live in Stockbridge, where you could always hear the train rolling through the yard. He knew if he stayed he would either kill somebody or get killed himself. One day he just felt his time had come. His mother knew he was preparing to go some day, and even though she didn't want him to go, he knew she wouldn't have stood in his way. One day, he knew it was his time, and he just walked out of the house and jumped on a train. That train carried him to Atlanta.

There was another silence. A memory of my own father flashed through my mind. His father's father, my grandfather, had died when my father was a boy, and somehow my father pulled himself out of the poverty he was thrust into. He too had escaped. Now he had been dead for about ten years. I wished I could ask him how he had done it. He had tried to make a home for me so that I wouldn't have to escape by running away from home and jumping on a train. I admired my father more than any other man. I wanted to tell Reverend King about this, my story, but I never did.

The silence was long. Mrs. King had been walking around in her room for a while, and as her door opened, Daddy King looked at me and said, "You can't let them discourage you. You can't let them hold you back. Pick yourself up, Brewster. Pick yourself up."

10

The Drinking Gourd

I MET REGULARLY with the youth group over the course of the summer. We met on Sunday mornings for study and sometimes for the planning of events, and we met again during the week for fun and fellowship. Numbering between fifteen and twenty members, we never seemed to run out of things to do.

One evening I surprised them with what they thought was sheer wizardry. We had visited someone's house several miles outside of Atlanta, to the south. On our return home I drove the last car in our little caravan. The driver in the first car, coming to a T in the road, suddenly pulled over to the side. Thinking this to be something worth stopping for, they all got out of their cars, only to discover that the driver was lost. There ensued a debate among the other drivers concerning which was the best route back to Atlanta. The night was clear and the evening was warm, and no one seemed to be able to figure which direction would take us home.

Soon I stepped inside the circle and pointed toward the right. "That's the way," I said with confidence that surprised them. "Trust me," I said.

"But you've never been here," they replied.

"That's the right direction," I said walking back to my car. Soon everyone was back in their cars and driving off in the direction I had indicated. Skeptical about my confidence, but having no other plan, they were all willing to go along. Sure enough, within a mile or so we came across a sign for Atlanta.

"How did you know?" my passengers asked me, begging and begging for an answer.

I just responded with an all-knowing smile. "I just know," I teased. "I'm very wise."

When we arrived back at Ebenezer, everyone pooled around me, pulling at my shirt and trying to coax my wisdom from me.

"Okay," I said. They pulled back and waited for my answer. "Did you ever hear of the spiritual, 'Follow the Drinking Gourd'?" Most of them had heard of it. "Well, I followed the Drinking Gourd," I told them. I could see all this didn't help them much so I began singing the song:

> The old man is awaitin' to carry you to freedom
> Follow the Drinking Gourd.

They were as mystified as ever so I let my secret out. This song contained the code for the direction toward freedom. The Drinking Gourd — the Big Dipper — pointed to the North Star, and if you could find that star in the night, you knew which way to travel in the dark without a map. When I saw the Big Dipper, I found the North Star in the sky, and then I knew I could find Atlanta by going in the direction of the North Star. One arm of the T in the road pointed north, the other arm pointed south. So I suggested we take the road heading north. "Simple as that," I said.

I smiled to think that a spiritual had helped to guide our little caravan home, just as slaves had used the Big Dipper to guide them as they fled slavery under the cover of the clear night sky.

11

Oh, Happy Day

SHORTLY AFTER I arrived, the youth group informed me that one of their members was seriously ill in the hospital. I talked with Lillian and Sarah about this in the office the next day.

"Oh, honey," Lillian said, "that is too sad for words." She told me that Annette had been in the hospital for a number of weeks, but that her parents refused medical treatment for her. "They believe that if God wants her to live, God will let her live. They pray by her bedside, they pray at home, they pray in church, but that little flower droops more every day. Doctors say they could cure her, but her parents say it is in the hands of God."

I heard Sarah in the background say, "My, oh my."

I decided to call on Annette in the hospital. I found her in a small private room, lying in bed with a sheet loosely pulled over her. She was about thirteen or fourteen years old. Her eyes were open when I entered and she was gazing out the window at a pigeon walking back and forth on the window ledge. She rolled her head over when I entered and extended her hand as I introduced myself.

At this point in her illness she had lost a lot of weight. Her bare arm had little flesh and I could see the delicate bones under her skin. Though her eyes sparkled with life, they seemed to have fallen back deep into her head. She spoke in a clear but very soft voice. Every once in a while we paused in our conversation to watch the pigeon walking back and forth and to listen to its gentle cooing. I suggested that it had come especially to Annette's window ledge to bring the dove's greeting. She knew her Bible and quietly quipped, "It doesn't yet have an olive branch."

"The waters must have a little way yet to fall before the olive branch will come," I replied. It seemed that we could communicate more deeply in biblical metaphor than in simple sentences. I wondered, however, what she thought would happen when the olive branch appeared at last. Over what gangplank would she walk and to what shore would it bring her? During the course of our conversation she dropped hints to me in metaphor that seemed different from what she said to her parents, friends, and nursing staff, all of whom tried to cheer her up with happy talk about getting better and coming home.

Soon after I arrived, her mother entered the room. She went immediately to Annette and grasped her firmly by the hands as we introduced ourselves. She soon began to pray.

"Dear Lord, I know you will make Annette well. I know you want her to get better. You know she wants to join her friends and family. Please, please...." With this she paused and then quickly resumed again with prayers of assurance. The gentle Father knew best and would make her daughter well soon. I listened to her mother talk about all the happy things Annette could look forward to when she got better. Everything was going well and the good Lord knew best about her cure. I decided it was prudent to let them be together. Three's a crowd, I thought, in a room such as this.

"Look after the dove," I said to Annette as I left, as we heard the pigeon still cooing and saw it walking back and forth on the window ledge. Our eyes met.

"I'm waiting," she said.

"I am, too," I replied.

I paused at the nursing station and spoke briefly to the nurses. "No doctors are allowed to make a medical intervention," one said to me, shaking her head sadly. "She is such a sweet girl."

"Is there nothing to do?" I asked. She shook her head slowly. I stood there, simply taking it all in, before I thanked them and left.

A few days later I visited Annette's parents at their home. They were filled with hope and spoke glowingly of God's power to rescue his people and heal the sick. Brimming with confidence, they showed me the room they were preparing for Annette's return. Her bed was strewn with letters and with photographs of her family and friends, and dolls and teddy bears were propped up in playful embraces on the pillows.

"She will be so happy when she comes home," her father said, picking up a bouquet of flowers and bringing it to his lips. Then he invited me to pray for her. They took my hands and I began to pray, drawing on the ACTS prayer formula I had learned, basing my prayers on the words "adoration," "confession," "thanksgiving," and "supplication." The supplication part was more drawn out than usual as they joined their requests with mine. We were still for a moment before we broke the circle, and Annette herself seemed to be present in the silence.

I talked to many people over the next few days about Annette's condition. I even went to the hospital again and talked briefly with a doctor. Yes, he could help her — he could have helped her, he clarified — but soon it would be too late. I wondered if we could get a court order to release Annette from parental control. The doctor assured me they had thought of this, but that the process would take too long; she didn't have that much time. All that could be done was to try to make her comfortable.

In Annette's room, I found her drowsy. She knew I was there but said nothing.

"Where is the dove?" I asked.

"Searching for the olive branch," she whispered, smiling into my eyes. Then she shut her eyes. The room was full of the smell of flowers, which had been placed on every available surface, but it also smelled of sickness. I took her hand in mine and prayed before I left.

The next time I visited her, I could see that this beautiful drooping flower was drooping more and more. The pigeon was not at the window ledge; I missed its gentle cooing and bold strutting back and forth.

"Where is the dove?" I questioned. With some effort she turned on her side and whispered, "Still searching for the olive branch."

"Pray for me, Reverend Brewster," she said, taking my hand and squeezing it tightly. "I just like to hear your voice in prayer." She kept holding my hand, and when I had finished she squeezed it even more tightly than before. "Keep going," she whispered. "I love to hear your voice in prayer, just talking to God."

I began again, this time without my formula. I quietly talked to God, listened to Annette's breathing, and then talked some more. Somewhere in that prayer I sensed that she knew she was going to die. As I lingered there beside her, talking quietly, I was aware that she had called forth something far deeper in me than the prayer formula on which I had relied. As we held hands, we two were together in the presence of the Holy, simply talking and listening and acknowledging the presence of the Spirit and the fragility of life.

All at once, there was a knock on the door and her parents entered the room. Her mother walked right over to Annette and took her hand as I let it go. It felt as if she were taking Annette away from me. I backed off, letting the warmth of her touch slip away. I said good-bye and prepared to leave, wondering if I would ever see her again.

Turning her eyes from the empty window ledge back to mine, Annette whispered, "He will find it soon."

"That will be a happy day," I answered.

"Yes," she said, faintly whispering as her face suddenly brightened. "Oh, happy day."

12

Quit Your Gaping

THE ROUTE that I drove from Reverend King's house to Ebenezer took me past a public swimming pool. It was one of the hottest summers on record, and in the late afternoons the pool was always teeming with children of all ages. As I drove by, I could hear the joyful noises of children splashing and enjoying the summer fun. Their energy was contagious, and I would often slow my car down just to let all that youthful excitement race through me.

One day I pulled over. The sign read that it was a City of Atlanta pool, open to the public. A lifeguard was on duty, sitting high on his perch like a hawk on a telephone pole, scanning the life below. As I looked around, I could see no black children, and it occurred to me that black children might not be welcome. Perhaps they were not allowed into the pool. Perhaps not even through the gate. Yet the sign read, "Open to the Public."

As I sat there, I noticed a black mother with three children walking by on the other side of the street. As they got opposite the gate the oldest child, who was about ten, looked at the pool and all the children playing in it. He slowed his pace and gently tugged on his mother's dress.

"Quit your gaping," she said sternly, without looking at what her son was seeing. "Quit your gaping, Michael." Then she picked up her pace so that Michael had to run to catch up.

I watched that group of four until they rounded the corner. Michael's face was the last to disappear as he tried to catch one more glance at the white children swimming happily in the pool. I turned to watch the pool and all the white children swimming and splashing while all of Atlanta baked in the sweltering heat.

I opened my car door and walked slowly toward the lifeguard. I just wondered, and I was at least going to ask. As I approached, he looked down at me from his perch, which was high enough so that I felt small beside it.

"Is this pool open to the public?" I asked.

"Open to the public," he answered confidently. He was about twenty years old, darkly tanned, with a lifeguard's build, and as he spoke, I felt welcomed by his smile and the directness of his gaze. I could see the boys and girls having so much fun, and I wanted Laura, Ronald, Jack, and the others to join in the fun as well.

"I work with a church youth group," I said. He nodded his head as if to say no problem with that. "They are from Ebenezer."

"Where?" he asked.

"Ebenezer Baptist Church," I told him.

He turned in his seat and looked at me quizzically. "The one on Auburn Avenue?"

I nodded. "Yes."

He turned away, mumbling under his breath. A few moments passed before he turned back to me. "What the hell are you doing there?" he asked. "A bunch of niggers."

Stunned by his remark, I stood there for a moment as he turned his back on me and looked toward the diving board where kids were competing to see who could make the most perfect cannonball.

As I turned to face the lifeguard again, I noticed that two other lifeguards and an older man in street clothes were coming toward me.

"What's your question?" the older man asked.

"I work with a youth group from Ebenezer Baptist Church," I said, "and I wondered if I could bring them here to swim some afternoon."

"Here? Hell, no," he said, his jaw tightening as if to squeeze the words into projectiles so he could spit them at me.

"The sign says it's a public pool — open to the public," I replied.

"Not for niggers, it ain't," he shot back. A tension-filled silence followed.

I decided to press the point. "You mean in this heat you won't let Negro children swim in a pool paid for by public taxes?" I could feel my anger rising but I wanted to keep in control. A few children came around to see what the discussion was all about, and then some parents, mostly mothers, joined in. Surrounded by a mob again, I could clearly grasp the situation, but still I didn't want to back off. I looked at the older man, then at the lifeguard, and then at the parents.

"You don't want to let my kids swim in this public pool in all this heat? Don't you think they want to swim just as much as these white kids do?"

"If you want trouble, I'll call the police," he said, holding his ground and staring at me like someone in authority. By this time more than twenty people had surrounded me. I was not scared so much as angry.

I turned and walked slowly toward the group of mothers, through the point in the circle that I thought was the softest. They parted like the Red Sea. I paused in the midst of them. "This is cruel and outrageous," I said to the mothers as I passed through them on the way to my car. I walked slowly across the grounds, shaking my head and not looking back.

I was so angry that I could feel the flames of war heating up. I felt like bringing a big gang and beating the hell out of them in order to take over the pool for the black children of the city. I was enraged by the injustice that my youth group and all the other black kids had to suffer. Again I heard that mother say, "Quit your gaping" to her son who, tugging at her dress, was wondering in his ten-year-old heart why he couldn't swim in the pool with all the other children. "Quit your gaping," she had scolded, and her words burned into my soul.

"Okay, Michael," I thought, "let me gape for the two of us. Let me gape until I see the depths of human ugliness played out before my eyes for all to recognize. Let me gape until the hand of judgment thunders down into our midst. But then, now that I myself am gaping, O God, what should I do?"

13

Meeting with Dr. King Jr.

WHEN I STEPPED BACK and looked at my life during the first several weeks in Atlanta, I saw parts of my work going well and other parts going badly. I was surprised at my rejection by the white church and at the hostility of many whites. The incident in the gas station parking lot made me realize how vulnerable I was, and my experience at the swimming pool left me feeling angry and raw. I had seen hatred in the people's eyes — hatred such as I had never seen before. More than two dozen pairs of eyes wanted me, so it seemed, either dead or far away, so that my question would never be posed to them again. I remembered my own intense rage and the animosity I felt toward that group of mothers. Suddenly I had found how easy it was to hate and how consumed I could become with hating people. That realization caught me by surprise.

The situation "out there" was far worse than I had imagined from reading reports up north about southern racism. If I was honest with myself, I would have to admit that I was filled with fear and immense anger, and I was in deep despair and frustration over my inability to accomplish any of my goals.

It was with great trepidation as well as excitement that I walked into the SCLC office and asked for Dr. King. His secretary, Dora McDonald, led me back to his office and soon I was seated comfortably beside him. I had so many questions and so many disturbing feelings that I didn't know where to begin, but he broke the silence.

"How are things going?"

"It's pretty bad out there." Having heard me talk about my experiences, he nodded slowly. There was a silence as he studied my expression. After a pause, I dove right into my disturbing questions. "How do you deal with your anger? How, when they hate you, do you keep from hating them back?"

He began to talk about hate and love. "Hate will build up in you until it explodes in violence. You must meet the force of hate with the force of love, or you will be consumed by hatred. You must meet the force of hate with the force of love." It was hard for me to imagine how I could do that.

"You have three choices," he continued. "Only three. You can adjust yourself so that you go along with their oppression and hatred, like the Hebrews speaking out against Moses because they would rather resign themselves to oppression than struggle for their freedom. Or you can fight violence with violence, but an eye for an eye leaves everyone blind. The way of violence is both impractical and immoral. It seeks to kill people, not convert them. It leaves bitterness and brutality in its wake." I had read some of these words in his writing before, but hearing him say them directly to me carried tremendous force.

"But there is a third way — nonviolent resistance. Nonviolent resistance against evil." Evil must be resisted, he explained. The struggle is against the evil system, not against those corrupted by the system.

"How did you get to that position of nonviolent resistance?"

He had started in Montgomery by emphasizing Christian love. The Sermon on the Mount guided him. It was those words of Jesus that first inspired blacks in the Montgomery bus boycott. Soon Gandhi's ideas made sense. Not passive

resistance but nonviolent resistance to evil. The one who passively accepts evil is as guilty as the one who perpetuates evil.
The aim was not to defeat and humiliate white people but to
win them over to friendship and understanding. Nonviolence,
in the last analysis, is not a technique or a strategy; it is a way
of life.

"Passive resistance," he added, "is easily misinterpreted, as
if it were merely passive, not requiring courage and strength.
Some people always find it easier to pick up the gun."

I wondered if I had it within me to change so completely,
to turn my hatred and anger into love, to turn my temptation to violent action into acts of compassion, to turn my
search for an effective strategy into a way of life. How could
I accomplish that?

"You must get discouraged," I said. "How do you keep from
discouragement and despair?"

"You have to decide whose work this is. Is it your work or
God's work? If it is just you," he went on, "then when the
road gets too steep you stumble and fall and turn back. If it
is God's work, you're part of a larger force for good. You meet
setbacks with calm assurance. You believe you are part of a
larger purpose."

"Is that what happened to you that night in Montgomery
when your house was bombed?" I asked.

"Yes," he said. Then he told me about the crisis that
changed his life. His house was bombed; he was at the end
of his powers. "I just told God I was afraid. I couldn't face
the struggle alone." Suddenly, he said, he felt the presence of
God. And he heard a voice saying, "Stand up for righteous-
ness. Stand up for truth, and God will be at your side forever."
After that he was ready to face anything.

There was a long pause. There was so much I wanted to ask.
He broke the silence again. "Remember," he said, "the struggle
is not against bad individuals. It is against evil systems." He

spoke of segregation and how it affected passengers who rode the bus to and from work each day. Good people get caught up in evil systems and act in evil ways. If you use one evil system to fight another, all you do is compound the evil in the universe. When he spoke about confronting evil his voice began to rise.

"How do you break the power of evil?" he asked. "Only with the power of good." He paused again. "It is never the right time for an evil system to change. Change is always too fast. Change is always at the wrong time. Slow down — did those churches tell you that?"

"Yes," I answered. "They told me we were going too fast."

"Well," he said slowly, "but we've been waiting a long time."

"You talk about suffering," I said. "Suffering is part of the struggle, isn't it?"

"With a powerful agenda you need a place for human suffering," he said. He then spoke slowly about suffering in the course of the struggle. Suffering for the sake of the good. Redemptive suffering. Suffering with Jesus in the suffering of the world. I could feel that he spoke out of his own pain.

"They don't teach much in seminary about suffering for some higher cause, do they?" he asked, laughing.

"I haven't heard about that yet," I told him, amazed myself at how little my educational experience had prepared me for such a struggle.

"But it's not all suffering," he said with a laugh.

As we stood up to shake hands, he thanked me for the work I was doing. "I enjoyed the talk," he said. "We'll talk again." We said good-bye and I emerged from the cool SCLC offices into the heat of Auburn Avenue. I turned left and walked slowly up Auburn toward Ebenezer.

I was in a kind of shock. I felt inadequate to meet the great challenges ahead. I had studied Christianity for years, and yet I knew nothing about the most basic things. All this talk about justice, and I knew nothing about what is involved in bringing justice about. All this study about love, and I knew nothing about loving enemies. I had no real enemies. If I was sheltered from enemies in my life and in my education, how could I ever get training that would show me how to love my enemies? Passing exams and studying was such an individual matter; how could I learn about evil systems and about confronting systems instead of individuals?

With all this high, heady talk about Jesus' suffering, I really knew nothing about my own suffering. Had I ever suffered in fighting for a larger cause? Had I ever shared my suffering with anyone? Had anyone ever linked my suffering to the redemptive suffering of Jesus? There was so much I wanted to learn. Who could teach me about this part of Christianity?

Very slowly I continued up Auburn Avenue, just wanting to walk and keep walking. I turned away from the direction of Ebenezer and walked and walked. I had been so sheltered in my life and so protected. And while the Christianity I was learning at seminary was infinitely fascinating intellectually, it seemed to make little difference in the actual world, where people lived and died, and where they struggled for justice and suffered long and hard without reprieve. After hours on the street in the heat of the city, I finally turned toward Ebenezer. I felt that a voice had reached deep into my soul, calling me toward transformation and toward a way of life that would bring out the best in me and hopefully the best in others.

Suddenly this felt like real education. The classroom was right before my eyes. I was an eager student, and my teachers were opening up new worlds and inviting me to join them. They were seeing a new Brewster, one I hadn't known before, and they were opening wide the door for this new Brewster to enter.

14

Singing for Freedom

OVER THE COURSE of these first few weeks I had be-friended a man named Bill, a member of Ebenezer, who planned to enter the ministry. He was about my age, and he had been involved in the protests in Atlanta. Eager to show me around, one day he asked me to go with him to a church meeting in preparation for the training conference on nonviolent resistance Dr. King had invited me to attend in Alabama. I accepted eagerly, and soon we were driving across town.

The church was a little smaller inside than Ebenezer. People had already gathered and were singing "Go Down, Moses" as we entered. As we took our seats as unobtrusively as we could, people all around the church began to look at me. I suddenly noticed that I was the only white person among the two hundred or so people in the congregation. The singing almost came to an awkward halt as we sat down. Sensing this awkwardness, Bill got up and spoke to one of the ushers. The usher went forward and said something to the leader, who listened with downcast eyes. All at once he looked up and gave me a warm, welcoming smile. I could hear his voice above the others, singing, "Way down in Egypt's land," and led by his strong voice, the vigorous singing of the congregation once again filled the church.

After my initial embarrassment subsided, I became aware that I was sitting next to a large woman. Seeing the leader's welcoming smile, she reached out and took me by the hand. "Welcome," she said. Others around her followed her lead, and in the midst of all the singing, I greeted them in return.

At the final words, the leader began to sing alone, "Let my people go," and the congregation echoed, "Let my people go." Back and forth they went. With each coupled refrain the singing grew more impassioned and the music more complex. All at once I could feel the spirit rising. The woman beside me stood up and raised her hands in the air, and others in the congregation stood up too, closing their eyes and swaying to the rhythm. I had never experienced such singing. Then the singing grew softer and finally stopped, leaving the piano's mellow chords to cradle the soft responses of the people.

The leader walked to the podium and began to pray. He prayed about the new Exodus, the new Israelites, the new Promised Land, and the new freedom to which Jesus was leading them, and as the piano played quietly on, the congregation responded in all the variations that spring spontaneously from the heart: "Yes, Lord," "Thank you, Jesus," "Lead us, Jesus," "Yes, yes."

I felt deeply alone and uncomfortable. This wasn't my style of worship. How could I stand up and raise my hands in the air and sway to the music with my eyes closed? How could I give verbal responses while the leader was praying? It seemed that all eyes were watching me, the only white person there, to see if I was with them or not, judging by how I moved my body. Even as I felt the intensity building in my own spirit, I asked myself, What am I really doing here? Am I nothing but a tourist gawking at the longings of strangers, intruding upon a solemn gathering? Would they think of me as a parasite coming to soak up their life's energy because I had none of my own?

Meanwhile, my neighbor's large left arm was pressing me into my seat as she swayed with the rhythm of the music.

From time to time she pushed hard against me, apparently without realizing it, and I knew I couldn't climb over her to leave, dragging Bill behind me. My hand still throbbed with the feeling of her powerful welcoming handshake. Part of me knew that I didn't belong there at all, but another part responded to the heat of the spirit pressing deeply into my flesh. Instead of crowding and pushing me away, the pressure from her arm against my body brought us together physically and spiritually, and although she rarely looked at me, I felt connected to her pulsing energy.

After the prayer, the leader spoke about their ancestors' struggle for freedom. The struggle today carried forward the struggles of the generations that came before them, he said. The suffering of those previous generations was calling out to this generation to struggle in our own day so that today's people could live in the Promised Land that their ancestors had yearned for but had never seen.

"The living spirits are rising up from the unmarked graves of the countless dead and calling out to us to march on toward the prize of freedom and never give up." I could feel that the power of this yearning came from the blood of ancestral suffering blended with the suffering of the present day.

But where did this leave me? I had never heard my family talk about the suffering of my ancestors. I knew of no great struggle for freedom that my ancestors had to endure, aside from the struggles of normal existence. When I sang "Let my people go," I wondered what I was really singing about. Part of my parents' struggle was to protect me so that I wouldn't have to suffer, and as far as I knew they had succeeded remarkably well. Maybe when the congregation sang "Let my people go," they were asking God to help them share the good life that I and "my people" had known.

My father, who died when I was fourteen, had often spoken about "keeping the wolf from the door." He had struggled with that wolf, which had burst through the door of his home when he was a boy. I was grateful that he had worked hard to keep the wolf away from my childhood door. I wondered, however, whether his success really kept me from singing that spiritual from my heart.

Let my people go from what? I asked myself. Was I not already living in the Promised Land? Did not the success of my father and mother and the apparent success of their ancestors go far to assure my safe crossing into the land of milk and honey? Did they not succeed in bringing me up on the happy side of the two great waters of freedom, the Red Sea and the Jordan River? What struggle was there for me to sing about? These and a bundle of other questions tumbled over and over in my mind as the leader prayed and the people sang.

A new person rose and came to the podium. He spoke about the struggle outside the doors, of danger and the need to sacrifice. He then described being in a lunch counter sit-in at a Woolworth's store in North Carolina. The congregation cheered as he declared that he and his friends were going back until either the jails were full or the lunch counters were open. I cheered along with them.

Why was the struggle for freedom so important to me? My mind jumped to the work I had done the year before with a black gang in Harlem. I had done my seminary field-work at the Morningside Community Center, and over time I had come to know several individuals and their families quite well. I could sympathize with those high school boys and girls when they looked toward their future with apprehension. I could feel the anger in their voices, in their music and dancing, in doors slamming and Ping-Pong balls smashing against the walls.

My high school education had taught me little of the struggles of people, but at Haverford College, which I had attended,

with its Quaker tradition, I had learned about Quaker aboli-
tionists and the many struggles for justice in which Quakers
routinely engaged. All these thoughts flew around in my mind
as I listened to the story of the lunch counter sit-ins. While
I wanted to apologize for my skin color, something told me I
belonged right there in the heart of the struggle, even if the
struggle was in part against the very system of privilege which
I had known and enjoyed.

The speaker ended amid cheers. I saw the pianist look in
my direction and nod slowly. My heart jumped. He eased into
some chords and a melody line slowly emerged. What was
going to happen next? Was he really looking at me?

Suddenly the woman on my right grabbed my hand and
gave it a terrific squeeze. Just as suddenly, she let it go and
stood up. The pianist was evidently looking at her, not at
me, and I felt relieved. She shut her eyes and began to sway,
feeling the music with her whole body. Her arms rose slowly
and a low hum came from deep inside her. Drawing a great
breath, she began to sing "Precious Lord" in a rich, powerful
voice. She sang slowly, each syllable carrying a heavy load of
meaning. When she got to "Take my hand," people began to
cheer. She leaned against me and then away and then back
again, her hands lifted and her eyes shut.

> Lead me on, let me stand;
> I am tired, I am weak, I am worn.

When she arrived at "I am worn," people responded with loud
applause.

> Through the storm, through the night,
> Lead me on to the light.

> Take my hand, precious Lord,
> Lead me home.

At the end of the first verse, the pianist played with a dramatic flourish, gradually quieting down and slowing his pace as he prepared for her entrance into the second verse. I felt chills up and down my spine. Had I been sitting alone in a dark corner, I would have let my tears flow down my cheeks, but as it was I was too afraid to move or show my feelings. After the second verse the pianist again began to improvise, but this time it was longer and he didn't slow down. Finally he nodded to my neighbor and she picked up his rhythm, singing the third verse at a much faster tempo.

> When the darkness appears
> And the night draws near
> And the day is past and gone,
> At the river I stand;
> Guide my feet, hold my hand.
>
> Take my hand, precious Lord,
> Lead me home.

By the time she reached the end everyone was standing up, some shouting, others clasping the hands of their neighbors and waving them over their heads. The pianist carried this emotion for a time. Finally he gradually reduced the intensity of his playing until all the people sat down.

Then the leader returned to the podium and introduced another speaker. "Let us hear from our brother about the Freedom Rides in Alabama and the struggles in our neighboring state."

"The struggle is hard out there," the new speaker began. In his mid-twenties, he had been involved in the Freedom Rides earlier that summer and also in the sit-ins in Greensboro, North Carolina, as well as other places some months before. He was tall and strong looking and he spoke with the authority of one who had been there. He described the scene: blacks returning hatred with love, amid curses and threats, answering violence with courageous acts of nonviolence. They were prepared to wait forever until they were served, just as the white people were served who sat right next to them. Everyone listened intently. He talked about how important singing was to the movement and what it was like to sing while sitting at the lunch counters, sing while they were being crammed into the police wagons, and sing while languishing in jails.

Following his talk, he led us in singing many freedom songs: "We Shall Not Be Moved," "Woke Up This Morning," "I'm So Glad," "Ain't Goin' to Let Nobody Turn Me Around," and "Keep Your Eyes on the Prize." Some songs referred to a person and a local event, such as Rosa Parks and the Montgomery Freedom Rides. Others dealt with recent events such as the sit-ins that occurred several months before. It was a teaching session that reflected the speaker's conviction that everyone committed to the struggle could be uplifted by singing.

All these songs focused on freedom — freedom now, not in the distant future and not in life after death. Hope was tangibly in the air. It wouldn't be the sweet chariots swinging low that would carry them home but the passionate effort of the people themselves, which would not be stopped. This new freedom rose up from the great struggle of the people, whose passionate faith told them that this time nothing would turn them around. When we sang "We Shall Not Be Moved," we could see in our minds angry white policemen with billy clubs coming at us. We could feel handcuffs and leg irons, and we could smell the awful stench of the jails. And always, the horrifying specter of the lynching tree somewhere off in the distance, beyond the law, this, too, was in our minds.

Although I sang with great energy, I still wondered what I was doing in that church. What would freedom look like for me? In seminary we had used such phrases as "freedom in Christ" and "Christ shall set you free," and we had studied Paul's ideas on the subject in his letters. But these words always seemed disconnected from history, disconnected from experience. My skin color and my economic status seemed to lift me outside the present struggle for freedom about which I sang.

Yet the singing touched me to the core. How could I rest easy, across the river in my Promised Land alone, and forget the others, scrambling over one another, trying to reach the shore on which I stood? The privileges that I had grown up with, the privileges I had not earned, did not exempt me from standing with people who were trying to lift the burdens of disadvantage from poor blacks and whites. I felt bonded to them. I would not be truly free until all the people singing with me were free as well.

Again the piano was heard, and upon hearing the music, everyone stood up one by one. Right arm over left, arms linked and bodies joined all around the room, we slowly started to sing. We sang softly at first, but by the time we sang "We shall overcome some day," everyone was singing out of their depths. Tears streamed down my face, and because both of my hands were being tightly squeezed from either side I simply had to let them flow and roll down my cheeks. "We shall overcome. We'll walk hand in hand. We are not afraid. The Lord will see us through. Black and white together. . . . Oh, deep in my heart, I do believe, We shall overcome someday."

Verse after verse, the whole body of the people leaned first to one side and then to the other, swaying to the music of freedom, to the music of hope.

When the singing was over, the woman next to me said, "Thank you for coming." She began to wipe the tears from her cheeks with a white handkerchief. Then, seeing that I had no handkerchief of my own, she wiped my face dry.

"Thank you," she whispered. "You helped me sing for my daddy and for my mummy and for my granddaddy and my grammy, and for all the people who lifted their souls up to God and sang for freedom, all those people who never got where they wanted to go, all the way back to the boats. May God love ya for singing tonight, and may you never stop singing for freedom."

The large woman still pressed against me in the crowded pew. Where our bodies met, our sweat on this terribly hot night was soaking our clothes. The leader returned and in a commanding voice said, "Jesus."

I waited for something to follow, but there was a long silence. What was happening?

"Yes, Lord," the woman spoke, quietly at first, and then louder so everyone could hear. "Yes, Jesus."

Then the leader began to pray. He prayed about Jesus who was in the front line of the struggle and was so liberated in his freedom that nothing could turn him around, nothing could take his mind off the prize, even when he faced Pilate and the Roman soldiers. Still he felt the suffering of the oppressed and suffered with them and for them. "Black and white together," he said.

Suddenly I felt welcomed into the sacred company of all those of every race who struggled for freedom. So quietly that I thought no one heard, tears welling up in my eyes, I whispered, "Yes, Jesus." But my neighbor must have heard me, for she responded, "Thank you, Lord." I leaned against her huge frame, our sweaty bodies communing in prayer.

Who that woman was, I never discovered. The evening was over and then it was time to go. All at once she had disappeared into the night. For days after that I heard the music of her soul and felt the heat of her arm against mine, molding the swaying of my body into my singing for freedom.

15

Schooling and Education

ON SATURDAYS, when there was a sense of leisure around the house, I frequently made pancakes for our breakfast. I woke up early, let Tappy out to recapture his domain from the squirrels, and settled into my chair with my reading and my journals. When I first heard Daddy King stirring upstairs, I put some bacon on to sizzle and crackle, and soon the pancakes were cooking nicely in the skillet.

Daddy King had hinted several times about his experiences in school and I was eager to explore this part of his life in more detail. When we had polished off our first round of pancakes and bacon and were settling in to a more relaxed pace of eating, I asked him about it.

His father had no interest in his schooling, he told me. He saw no future in it for a sharecropper's son. His father thought that his job was to raise him to be a sharecropper just like himself and to teach him to be content walking all day behind a mule. He wanted to teach his son about raising animals, working the land, and dealing with white folks. But Daddy King saw that there was no future for him in harvesting cotton for a white man's profit.

"My father lived so he could get just enough change at the end of the year to buy himself some hope. My mother," he said, "was different." She couldn't read or write but "every chance she got, she pushed me out the door and off to school."

He paused for a moment. I wondered what memories were flooding his mind. "What was your school like?" I finally asked.

"It was an old shack," he said. He remembered one fall when it rained a lot, his teacher, Mrs. Low, put a bucket beside his desk to catch the drops from the roof so that his feet wouldn't get wet. He had no books, no blackboard to write lessons on, no materials. Nothing but a teacher and a few students sitting in old rickety desks that had been discarded by the white children's school on the other side of town.

When he was in school he wasn't doing chores around the farm, so his father made sure the chores were done before he went. That meant he got up early. "I worked so hard that I carried the smell of the barn right into school." At that moment, his right hand began to move in a rhythmic motion.

"What are you doing?" I asked.

He looked off into the distance. "I used to curry the mule. Every morning. Now, that was something I loved to do." I sensed that he had deep feelings about that mule, but I let them rest. His thoughts continued about his teacher.

Mrs. Low, the wife of the preacher at Floyd Chapel, was his only teacher during his early schooling. From her he learned that there was something beyond the farm, beyond Stockbridge. She told stories. On some days, the students would leave their desks to go outside and sit at her feet under a big old tree in the shade and she would just start talking. There was a train that rolled through Stockbridge several times a day. She awakened their imaginations and put them into an imaginary train, and in that train she took them all over the world. That train took them to New York, Chicago, Detroit, and San Francisco. "All over," he said. "She filled up my imagination until I thought it would burst."

She talked about history, Cleopatra and Caesar. He remembered one winter when she got them to come back to school at night to see the stars. She showed them the planets and

the Milky Way. Then she showed them the Big Dipper. She
called it the Drinking Gourd. It pointed to freedom. He said
he never forgot that North Star. You walk in that direction,
he described Mrs. Low saying, and sooner or later, if you are a
slave, and you travel at night so you won't get caught, you'd
cross the river over into the Promised Land. She had known
people who had done that, and she spoke of them with such
respect that to his little mind they seemed like gods and god-
desses. He went home and his head was swelling with wonder.
"I loved school, but I could only go two or three months of
the year. I had too much work to do helping my father on the
farm."

He paused and looked into the distance. "Those were hard
times, Brewster," he said at last. I wanted to hear more about
his life in Stockbridge, but he seemed reluctant to go on.

"How did you get to Atlanta?" I asked.

"One night I just made up my mind, and I went down to
the railroad yard and slipped into a boxcar. The next morning
I was in Atlanta." He got a job cleaning up the railroad yard
and earned good money. He was fourteen but told them he
was twenty. He was big for his age so no one questioned him.
"Every time I turned around I was told 'nigger do this, nigger
do that.' " They didn't bother with his name.

He was getting on pretty well when one day his mother
came into the railroad yard and grabbed him by the wrist.
"Right here," he said, showing me where she had grabbed him.
"She hauled me away." That hurt, he said, but he wasn't going
to disobey his mother. He never got paid what he was owed.
After that, he stayed on the farm until he was eighteen, working for his father. "My father's life was all about tomorrow.
Tomorrow this and tomorrow that, but his tomorrow never
came for him the way he hoped it would. His tomorrows were
all his yesterdays, just stretched out into the future."

His mother told him once that if ever he were going to leave home, she'd be all right. She sensed something in him that was not made for the farm. "She kind of pushed me along way out beyond herself."

He paused for a moment. A few years ago, he went on, he went to Paris, and he spent a quiet moment thinking of Mrs. Low.

"She had taken me to Paris in my imagination, as a boy. When I was plowing behind our mule, I would think of Paris, London, and Rome. From beside that little shack of a school and under that old tree, she took me all over the world. And there I was, visiting Paris where she had never been. God love her."

When he was nineteen, he was back in Atlanta where his sister, Woody, now resided. She told him he had to go to school, even though it was elementary school, and she took him to Bryant Preparatory School where he would enroll for study.

"I thought I was pretty smart," he said. "I always liked numbers. But when I took the tests, the principal told me I had to start back in the fifth grade. In all my schooling, Mrs. Low had only brought me up to the fifth grade. Those were some of the hardest days of my life. Picture me, almost twenty years old, and having to sit with the fifth-graders." He couldn't even read the books they were reading, and he was too big for the desks. He was humiliated. He wanted to quit.

"I thought the mountain was just too steep," he said, but Woody kept telling him he couldn't get anywhere in Atlanta without an education.

Soon he began to work, he said, and he worked twice as hard as anybody else did. He worked on his lessons all day and all night, he had so much catching up to do. One day his mother and father appeared with an old car. "My mother had sold our cow to help buy me a Model T Ford. I was the happiest boy alive. From time to time I would drive home."

He paused, as if considering whether there was something more he wanted to say. "Are you talking about my schooling or my education?" he asked.

"About both," I said. "Tell me about your education."

"My education wasn't always what I wanted. It came right out of pain. But it made me a man."

One day his principal, Mr. Clayton, took him out of class and said that his father was in Mr. Clayton's office. He saw his father there and knew he had been drinking. His father wanted him to come home with him. " 'You're coming home with me, boy. I am your father and I need you. I can't do it alone any more.' " Daddy King looked at Mr. Clayton and Mr. Clayton looked right back.

"I could tell he wasn't going to say anything. He just looked at me and waited. How could I decide? I couldn't go back to the farm, but there was my own father needing me."

"What did you say?" I asked.

"I said, 'I can't go with you, Papa.' My father responded with a few words. 'I just can't go,' I said again. 'My future is here in school.' He stood looking at me. The silence almost broke my spirit. Then he just turned around and left. I can hear his footsteps to this day, walking away. I just stood there listening to him slowly walk away from me.

"Now that was education, Brewster. I had to decide right then about my life and my future. He walked away and I had to go back and sit with the ten- and twelve-year-olds. I couldn't even keep up with them in their studies. But nothing was going to keep me away from my education."

Suddenly the phone rang and Mrs. King called him to take the phone. My mind shifted to my own education. My real education might have started some thirty-five years before I was born, probably out of another moment of pain — my father's pain. He was in the eighth grade when his father died, leaving his mother, his aunt, and his sister without any means to support themselves. His only choice was to leave school and try to support them. So he left school and went to work as a messenger boy in a law firm, carrying papers around New York City. A few years later, he became a clerk in a law firm.

My mother told me that my father became a lawyer without going to law school. As a clerk, he read strenuously at night preparing himself to pass the bar exam. After passing the exam, he was admitted to the bar when he was twenty-four. One day my parents were attending a dinner for the lawyers of the firm and their wives. A man with an accordion was circling the tables, playing the college song of each partner. My mother wondered what my father would say when his turn came up.

"Mr. Brewster, what is the song of your alma mater? What shall I play for you?"

"East side, west side, all around the town," was my father's response.

He got his education on the sidewalks of New York. As a consequence of his lack of formal education, he wanted the best education possible for my brother and me, so he sent us to the best private schools he could find. I always admired him for pushing us forward into what he never had.

When Daddy King returned, I told him about my father's education in the streets of New York. He had a great laugh at the college song story, but I never told him how easy it was for me to go through grade school and high school with everything all paid for and with the encouragement of my parents. On the other hand, I never had a Mrs. Low to help my imagination soar beyond what seemed possible. I sensed that I had actually been limited by what my schooling had hoped for me. Perhaps I had been too well protected from struggle and pain.

"You can mention something about me," Mrs. King said with a chuckle as she passed by.

"I met Bunch," said Daddy King (he always called her Bunch), "when I returned to Atlanta, and it was what you'd call love at first sight." But how could he have a relationship, he wondered, with the daughter of one of the most prominent ministers in the city? He was the son of a sharecropper and he didn't deserve even to be in the fifth grade. He had to get some education so he could talk to her in good English, so she wouldn't think of him as just a farm boy. "If I was going to keep my eye on her, I had to keep my eye on a diploma."

"Who helped you most in school?" I asked, wondering if there was someone who looked after him in a special way.

"You could say it was Mr. Clayton, the principal. I learned from him that I could be somebody. Get that little, little piece of paper that said you passed, get out into the city to vote." He paused a moment reflecting. "Mrs. Low sent my imagination out and away from the farm to the world beyond, and Mr. Clayton took me from being a nobody to being a somebody. He told me how to vote and make a stand for what is right."

Back then Daddy King drove a truck to pay his bills at the rooming house. Nothing could stop him from getting that little piece of paper. He thought his schooling was over when he got his diploma, but Bunch made it clear to him that if he was going to be somebody he had to go to college. "She had already graduated and was kind of pulling me along."

He paused, looking me straight in the eye. There was a fierceness and power in his gaze. "We're talking education now, Brewster. My education was about struggle. It was one thing learning how to walk behind a mule on another man's land and pick cotton for another man's profit, and even learning how to deal with white folks, but going to school was a struggle."

He tried to get into Morehouse, but they looked at his tests and said he couldn't do the work. "I wasn't college material, they said. But I was so determined and stubborn that I just wouldn't take no for an answer." He walked into the office of the college president, Mr. Hyde, and somehow convinced Mr. Hyde to take a chance on him. "I bumped into a forest of people saying no, but it just took that one person to say yes."

He worked harder than anyone he knew, just to prove to himself he was college material. He flunked a lot of classes. "My goodness, I knew how to flunk classes," he said with a big laugh. Nevertheless, he finally got through. "There were no excuses for me. I had to make it on my own or I was through and out the door."

When he went courting Mrs. King, he had to get on with Reverend Williams, her father. "Oh my, he was a formidable man. I was pretty proud of myself, just finishing high school and going to college, but that wasn't good enough for him. 'A man has to have a mission in life,' Reverend Williams told me. 'A man has to be about something important.' He told me that my education had to have a mission behind it. A college diploma was not enough."

"Imagine what your father and mother would think of you today," I mused, astonished at what he had accomplished.

"I think of them very often," he said. "My mother pushing me toward an education she never could have herself, but she just knew it was the door that would take me out of sharecropping. My father was a smart man on the farm and I learned a lot from him, too. He had a lot of dreams but he never could get there. I learned that lesson as well. Wishing for tomorrow don't make it happen today."

He grew quiet. I thought I saw tears in his eyes as he looked out the window at Tappy chasing the squirrels. "Mrs. Low," he finally said, looking away. "What that woman did for me no one will ever know. Went to her grave trying to bring a little

light into the darkness of the lives of all those boys and girls
that were still out there on the farms, in a system that would
keep them down forever. There are a lot of Mrs. Lows in this
world, and thank God there was one for me. I'm still riding
her freight train. I heard that whistle, jumped on board, and
the Good Lord carried me away.

"I wish I could thank her," he said. "Some day I will."

16

You Call That Fishing?

⤾

"JUST TELL THEM, Lillian, I've gone fishing," I said as I was leaving the church office.

"Okay, Rev. I'll tell them our fishin' preacher has gone fishin'."

I walked across the street to the gas station where Smitty was waiting for me. "Just show up at nine o'clock," he had said. "You needn't bring any lunch; I'll take care of that."

The day was already hot and muggy and we knew it would be another scorcher. I walked to Smitty's car, where he was arranging rods in the trunk. We greeted each other warmly, and he showed me his tackle packed in boxes in the trunk.

"We've got plenty of hooks, plugs, and enough worms for a week," he said. "I've put together twenty-six rods and bobbers. That should do." I looked over the bobbers. Most of them were red and white while some were a lively mixture of yellows, blues, and greens.

At that moment, Smitty's son, Jack, a member of my youth group, came bounding out from behind the building. Rushing up to me, he shook my hand. "Ever been fishing before?" he asked.

"Yeah," I said. "Done some up north. Never like this, though. Do you use all these rods?"

"Sure do," Smitty replied proudly. "We need them all. Worms for every one. You just never know what hook a fish will take a hunger for." He packed our lunch in the trunk, sorted a few things, and soon we were pulling out of the gas station lot and heading away from Ebenezer and Atlanta.

It wasn't long before we were out in the country, the highways slowly turning into smaller roads and the smaller roads turning into back roads and the back roads turning into dirt roads with ruts.

I was used to streams that held some good pools for trout, and rivers that tumbled over stones and around boulders. I knew the feel of a light rod and the touch of a number sixteen fly on the surface. Here, however, the streams moved slowly, if at all. They seemed dark and foreboding. Some weeks before, they told me that a body had been thrown off a bridge into the inky blackness of a stream like the ones we were driving over, As we passed over bridges and beside the streams I wondered what mysteries these waters contained. We made several turns along a lightly traveled road and finally reached a lake. There we stopped, in the shade of a tree.

I watched closely as Smitty and Jack assembled their equipment along the shore. Their rods were about five or six feet long, each with its line and bobber. I hadn't fished with a bobber since the fifth grade, when I went to a summer camp, and I had never fished with more than one rod at a time.

After carefully putting a worm on each hook, they tossed them out as far as they could, with enough line below the bobbers so that the worms dangled a few inches off the bottom. Then they propped the rods on a rock, letting the line gently sag from the tip to the bobber before it vanished in the murky shallows. If they found no suitable rock, they laid a rod on the bank and let the line go out into the water from the tip. They fished in about five to eight feet of water, Smitty told me, as he walked along the bank setting up his rods. The process took about half an hour. I helped where I could, untangling the lines, putting worms on hooks, and tossing out the bobbers. Then we all went under the tree and sat down to wait.

We focused intensely on the bobbers spread out in front of us. Soon one of the bobbers dipped into the water. Jack sprang up and gave his rod a sharp jerk, but nothing was there.

"Stole my worm," he said in disbelief, as if to say, How could a fish do this to me? He reached into the worm can and re-baited his hook.

Every once in a while a bobber bobbed and there was a rush to the rod and a quick jerk. Most often this was followed by a disappointed gasp. Working smoothly in tandem, Jack supplied the speed and Smitty the direction, eagerly pointing his finger and shouting, "Over there," "Look at that," "Run, Jack," or "You've got to be faster." A quantity of worms was feasted upon before we landed our first fish, just before lunch. It was a little fish, measuring about eight inches.

"A keeper," was the happy consensus of my companions. "If we catch more, this will be our dinner," Smitty said. "One before lunch is good luck."

We lunched on bologna sandwiches, pop, cupcakes, and a few peanuts that Smitty's wife had put up for us. "Time for a little nap," Smitty announced after he had eaten his last peanut.

He was asleep when I landed my first fish. He rolled over, opened one eye, and confirmed the catch. "Nice one," he muttered. I took it off the hook and put it in the pail. "That's two."

For the next hour or so Jack and I watched the bobbers floating on the gentle waves as we looked out over the lake. Once in a while he rushed down to a rod only to find the worm gone. "There's one," "Oh, no, ate my worm," "Got him," "He got away," "Just a minnow," "Over there," "Run," "It's a keeper," "Lost him." Such was our talk on that beastly hot afternoon.

Finally Jack, too, said he was ready for a nap.

"You want me to watch the rods?" I asked. "All twenty-six of them?"

"Call me if you need me," he said. Soon both Smitty and Jack were asleep in the shade of the tree and I was left alone to keep an eye on the situation.

I could hear the sound of children swimming on the far side and could see several sailboats with bright-colored sails catching a distant breeze. It suddenly occurred to me that there were no black children playing in the water. What strange quirk of fate put those white children on that side in their sailboats, Smithy and Jack on this side, and me somewhere in between? How was it, I had wondered often in the past weeks, that I had slipped into their world so easily but they couldn't slip into mine; that I could move back and forth at will but they were fenced into their world? How unlike a fish that has the freedom of the water and can swim as it pleases from one shore to the other. Why did we create invisible fences that inhibit people on both sides? Why was I born with white skin, Smitty and Jack with black skin, and why did it seem to matter so much?

I was far away from my beloved trout holes, but I suddenly realized that I was enjoying myself — keeping watch while my friends slept, tending all their lines and bobbers, my heart warming toward them and their way of fishing. The sun was incredibly hot, but in the shade I found utter tranquility. Only now and then a fly landed on my face or an ant crawled up my leg. They had come to this shore to find a precious moment of life's peace and brought me with them. Let the bobbers bob, let the worms be devoured and the hooks re-baited, let a man's snooze wash over the struggles of living. At the end of the day they could go home with a few fish to grace their evening meal, and tell stories to an admiring audience of the day's great catch.

Beside this murky lake by which we found such pleasure, I questioned my life, asking myself the hard questions. Why had I been given so much? What is a person with so many advantages to do with one's life? Why don't more people try to right the wrongs of culture, level the playing fields, give the disadvantaged more of what they deserve? Why was it that my friends wanted to enter the corporate world that often seemed so destructive? Given the strange quirk of fate that was my birth, what was my life's calling?

My thoughts began to sail off in the breeze and build up like clouds as poetic lines began to fill my drowsy head:

Let the wild ways of heaven become infused in my
    bones.
O God, don't let them tame me.
Keep me from betraying my new vision of peace and
    justice,
and, please, in your Grace give me the courage. . . .

A bobber furiously jerking on the surface and then vanishing into the murky depths suddenly shook my reverie.

"Jack," I called, waking him from sleep. Together we rushed across the shore to where the rod was being dragged into the water. "Get him," cried Smitty, rolling over on one side to watch the action. Back and forth the great fish swam, snarling many of the other lines in a massive tangle. Jack furiously grabbed the rod and tried to drag the fish in to shore. Just as it flapped against the stones, Jack gave a huge jerk and the line snapped. We stood for a desperate moment, watching the monster swim slowly out of sight, dragging the bobber behind it. We were speechless.

"What a fish," Smitty finally said, rising to his feet and shaking his head. "What a fish. Never seen one like that here before."

We spent the next half hour untangling our lines. Every once in a while, Smitty broke the silence, "Never seen one that big before." As we sorted out the mess, Smitty told me how Reverend King had helped him start his gas station. "He thought I could run a gas station, and here I am, servicing a lot of Ebenezer's cars, doing some good, I hope." Then he turned his attention away from the bobbers. "It just doesn't matter if I catch something or not. Just having the chance of catching a fish gives me a reason to get away. Sitting on this shore, with my bobbers spread out in front of me, seems good enough. I come out here just to let things be. Seems like it takes real effort in this world just letting things be."

Smitty leaned back on his elbow and looked out over the water beyond the bobbers. "Got to know the back roads to catch fish," he said. "People see the lakes from the highways and imagine big fish lurking down in there. They follow tracks to the shore, but they catch nothing when there are tracks all around and crowds looking on. Got to learn the back roads. That's where you catch fish." He paused a moment and then looked at me. "Now, for you, coming to Ebenezer must have been like coming along a back road."

"Yes," I said.

"Like going where white folks hadn't been before."

People warned me not to come to Ebenezer, not to take this back road, I thought. But look what I found.

Another bobber bobbed and bounced in the waves. Jack was sleeping, so I started to get up, but Smitty put his hand on my shoulder. "Let it be. Maybe that's the monster's brother, but let him be. He deserves his freedom, too. I don't need him. Along the back roads, where nobody's watching, it's okay to let the big ones go. It's hard to let them go when a crowd is watching and egging you on."

On our way home, we sat mostly in silence. From time to time Jack recalled wistfully about the big one that got away.

"I keep the small ones and let the big ones be," Smitty mused, kind of to himself. When we arrived back at the gas station, people came out of nowhere and circled the car in excitement. "Hey, Smitty," they cried. "Let's see what you caught today."

"Just a few," he said, showing them his pail.

"Oh, what a catch." They all gathered around to get a good look. "Where is that lucky spot of yours? How do you get there?" Filled with envy, they tried to pry out of Smitty exactly where this coveted place was.

"Oh, it's out in the country a ways," Smitty casually noted as he and Jack arranged his rods.

"Sure like to try. Can you draw me a map?"

"Real hard to find," Smitty replied, still arranging his rods. "Don't know if I could draw you a map of how to get there. Got to find the right back roads. Easy to get lost. Might never find your way out. Dangerous."

The admiration of the bystanders was evident in their silence. They stepped back to let Smitty sort out his tackle. I could see that he was an admired man along this section of Auburn Avenue. He knew how to get out of town. He knew the secrets of the back roads. He knew how to keep his tracks hidden. He knew how to tell just enough of the story to keep the excitement buzzing. And he knew how to return for another catch. These things were worth watching, worth the admiration of the street.

"You call that fishing?" a guest at an ecumenical gathering of white clergymen challenged me a few days later, as I told the story of my day's fishing. I had been invited by one of those to whom I'd suggested the idea of holding a youth group conference at Ebenezer. Methodists, Presbyterians, and Episcopalians were represented there. Several of them came near to me to hear about my summer experience. Fresh from my day of fishing, I told them about my enjoyable hours with

Smitty and Jack and how I had learned to fish with twenty-six rods and bobbers.

Suddenly, a booming voice barged into the conversation, "You call that fishing? I'll tell you what fishing is." Everyone turned to listen. I saw immediately that this man was used to voicing his opinions while others stood passively by and listened. His laugh was full of sarcastic derision and the tone of his voice bit into me.

"Up in Labrador," he announced, "I killed five salmon in one day — setting the record for a day's kill that summer. You get one of those fish on your rod and you've got a fish. None of this twenty-six rods and bobber stuff." His voice was loud and condescending. "I wouldn't call that fishing if I were you. Maybe around the people of Ebenezer Baptist Church on Auburn Avenue, but not here. Not in this crowd."

I was speechless. My face reddened. The men around me laughed nervously, with a hint of approval, knowing exactly what he meant. But I was furious — furious at how he insulted Smitty, furious at how he ridiculed me, and furious at how he mocked the people of Ebenezer.

Seeing my reaction, the man added, "Oh, don't take it personally."

In my anger, I immediately wondered how I should treat this repulsive individual in the context of nonviolence? How should I stand up to these well-dressed, self-satisfied, arrogant white clergy who felt no anguish when they blatantly ridiculed blacks? I wanted to leave this group and go back to the sweet place by the peaceful lake with Smitty and Jack, quietly watching the twenty-six bobbers as we basked in the shade of a great tree.

"You can kill your salmon and make your records in the big rivers of Labrador," I finally said, "but I had a beautiful day with Smitty and Jack. And I call that fishing."

17

Make It Plain, Brother

"**I** ALWAYS LOVED the church," Daddy King said, "right from the time when I was a boy." His mother was a religious woman. "She was at peace with herself in troubled times," he said, "because she was at peace with God." Throughout those suffering times she was always led by the wisdom of the Lord. Whenever she could she took her son to Floyd Chapel, where Reverend Low was preacher.

"I owe a lot to my mother," he said. "She never fell into self-pity with all she lived through, because God always gave her the power to do what she had to do. She didn't get the rewards in this life...." He paused. "God love her," he finally said. His father resented his going to church, which he did whenever he could. "He was going nowhere and he wanted me to go right along with him." But inside the church he felt at home. It eased the pain.

Dr. King preached several times during the summer. I sat on the opposite side of the lectern from Daddy King, watching Dr. King lead the service. Hearing his slow, resonant voice calling people to worship, I reflected on the three generations of that family that had spoken from this very pulpit. Reverend A. D. Williams — (Mrs. King's father), Daddy King, and now Dr. King Jr. represented a powerful legacy of preaching. This preaching style was unlike anything I had known, so during another breakfast I asked Daddy King to tell me about his life as a preacher.

"I never got tired of going to revivals, with all that singing and preaching." He had a strong voice and he loved to sing. He could pick up any song they sang, and at an early age he began to sing in church. Back then, he told me, the singing carried the service along. And if you were a preacher it was good if you could sing. In those days, the preachers would come to those revival meetings on horseback. They called them Country Circuit Riders — C. C. Riders, for short.

"Back then, few people could read, and the C. C. Rider would make his reputation on his memory and his singing. Those old-time preachers could quote — not like today. For hours they would quote scripture, hours on end. Back then it was different.

"Well, I wanted to become a preacher, but the board of deacons at Floyd Chapel thought I was too young. At ten I knew God was calling me." He had to be passed by the deacons, by knowing scripture and preaching a trial sermon. When they didn't pass him, he went on singing. He began to learn, from the C. C. Riders and the old country preachers, the gestures and the rhythms of preaching.

"I would practice when walking behind the mule," he said. "Must have looked mighty funny, waving my arms and quoting scripture behind the mule. I had a good memory for scripture, and a lot of cotton fields heard a lot of scripture, a lot of preaching, and a lot of singing."

He wanted to be licensed, but they turned him down, "even though I knew more scripture than they did." He finally passed after he preached his trial sermon. "Papa made fun of me. But Mama was proud." He preached in those rural churches whenever they asked him to, so he got a lot of practice in rural settings. "When I sang, from an early age, I knew I could move people and touch their hearts so tears would flow down their cheeks. I found that I could move people with my preaching and really touch their hearts. What I mean is that I could bring the congregation to a fervor."

When he finally got to Atlanta, he let people know that he was a preacher. "I preached at a few churches," he said, "and I must have preached like those old C. C. Riders, because people were horrified. All this country stuff didn't go over to these city folks." That was when he was falling in love with Alberta Williams, the woman whom he would later marry, whose father was the well-known preacher at Ebenezer.

"Now, *he* was a preacher. His father had been a slave exhorter, a man who preached to the slaves, and he got his preaching ways from his father. I got my preaching ways from those old-time country preachers who knew their scripture and who tried to bring some dignity to those downtrodden country folk."

But he was in Atlanta then, and they rolled their eyes at his grammar and his country habits. He wanted to put these behind him forever because he realized that learning to preach by waving his hands, quoting scripture, and looking at a mule's tail all day was not the training he needed to be a city preacher. In Atlanta, the preacher needed to engage people's minds.

"Those were important years. I came to Atlanta wanting to curse whites for what they had done to Mama and Papa. 'Hatred only makes more hatred,' Mama would tell me. How could I keep my promise that I made to Mama, not to hate?"

In 1926, he got married and was preaching in two churches. He resisted becoming Reverend Williams's assistant when he was asked, because he wanted to make it on his own and not come in as the son-in-law. He preached at Travelers' Rest Baptist Church and another small church, but in 1931, when Reverend Williams died, the people of Ebenezer called Daddy King to be their pastor.

"Now, that was the Depression and those were hard times, but I preached Ebenezer through those years. The Lord was kind to us, upheld me in my struggle. You know, the people were so beaten down by white people that their faces were in the dirt. They came to church wanting to be lifted up in glory. Many of them came to church so angry at being treated like trash that it was all I could do to let them see the face of Jesus. I would get to church and just feel the anger burning."

He paused and looked directly at me. "Brewster, have you ever been called a nigger?"

"No," I answered.

"Well," he continued, "how do you preach to the soul of a man who has been called a nigger all his life and whose father and mother have been called nigger all their lives, and nigger is all they know? I see these men walking around the streets and walking in their sleep with their fists balled up. When their children come home and ask the question for the first time, 'What is a nigger, Daddy? Why do they call me a nigger?' you can feel hatred that's big enough to kill grow in their hearts. How do you preach to the soul of a man when he has no hope? How do you turn a man around to see love when he is full of anger? How to turn rage into hope? The preacher has a heavy burden."

Those were the days when people began to demand that something get done. They were getting fed up with talking. "Soon-ism became never-ism and I could feel their red blood boiling. I couldn't keep my mouth shut. So I preached. I preached loud enough so people could hear me. Even the Negro ministers told me to keep quiet when I preached about equal rights and voter registration. They didn't want me rocking the boat in the pulpit, but I raised my voice for the downtrodden. I preached the Word, and I tried to live the Word.

"I got tired, but you can't get tired enough to stop. You've got to preach to the pain of the people, and getting tired is part of the sermon. But you can't stop. Because now you're making history. I'm talking about the history Reverend Williams made. He caused a lot of things to change. I continued his legacy. I wanted to see God working now, not after all the people died. I wanted to see God working here and not in some far-off place."

He looked sternly at me, and with his eyes piercing my skin, he asked, "Where was the white minister who would stand up in his pulpit and preach the gospel? Where? They were afraid they would lose their churches if they preached the gospel, if they used their power to move the system. 'Niggers,' they would say, 'stay in your place. Don't agitate.' Would I stand up in the pulpit each Sunday and mimic the white preachers? No. I found justice in the scriptures and I had to preach the gospel."

It felt as if he was preaching to me. I wanted to say, "Yes, brother, preach. Make it plain. Preach to me," and encouraging statements like that, but suddenly he paused and became thoughtful.

"I met a lot of defeats in those days," he said, shaking his head. "God kept me going. He lifted me up. 'Don't stop now,' God would say. 'Too late to quit now, King.' "

He spoke with great admiration of Reverend Low in Stockbridge, preaching the Psalms, raising his eyes to the hills, and talking to God about freedom. "As I listened, I could see Papa walking the rows on a white man's land and Mama on her knees scrubbing the floor of a white woman's kitchen. In the street, people would call me 'nigger boy.' Here in my pulpit I was preaching God's freedom and justice. If I preached freedom and justice then I had to walk freedom and justice. A lot of times in those early days, in the 1930s, I walked alone. I received threats from white men who wanted to kill me, and I could look out over the people and feel the cold threat of being hung from a tree. You gotta walk the talk. That's too hard for most people. Too hard for most preachers. But it didn't stop me. Preaching the gospel is hard work because you've got to live it."

As I sat on the platform next to Daddy King and Dr. King, I imagined I could hear the cadences, see the gestures, perhaps recognize some of the words Reverend Low might have used in the rural churches so long ago. These cadences, gestures, and words Reverend Low would have learned from the preachers who had tried to bring the wisdom of scripture to people whose lives were filled with struggle, anger, and despair. As the Word was being preached right next to me, I sensed that a great tradition was being passed along, a tradition capable of lifting the spirit of a people high into the realms of glory. These were the cadences, the gestures, the words, and the passion that brought the blacks in Montgomery together and kept them walking over two winters, for 381 days; the cadences, the gestures, the words, and the passion that moved people to carpool to work, while the bus company refused to seat them in the front of the bus and while the white officials refused to negotiate.

At the height of his passionate oratory, it was as if I could hear the collective voices of Daddy King, Reverend Williams, Reverend Low, and the C. C. Riders from another time all calling out to Dr. King: "Preach it, Rev," "Yes, Lord," and "Thank you, Jesus," "Make it plain, brother."

Ebenezer Baptist Church in Atlanta, my home in the summer of 1961.

Me as a mere youth.

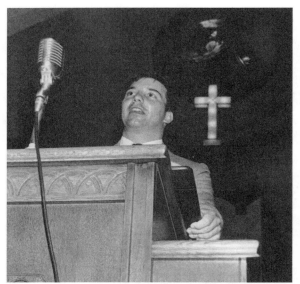

Preaching from the pulpit of Ebenezer.

With Martin Luther King Jr. in the church office.

Dr. King with his sister, Christine, and his mother, in his parents' back yard.

Me with Dr. King on the backyard swing.

Lillian Watkins and Sarah Reed, the church secretaries and office managers.

Some members of the Ebenezer Youth Organization (EYO).

Mr. Grimes, the custodian, with some of his children.

Smitty and me, two serious fishermen.

Martha Klippert, my future wife, during her visit to Atlanta.

Daddy King, after breaking his leg. Unfortunately the black-and-white photo doesn't show off his bright red pillow.

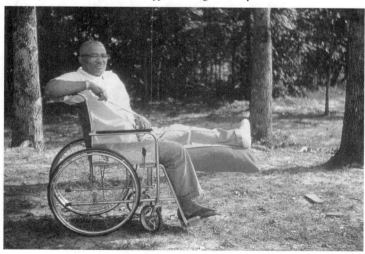

Greeting parishioners and saying goodbye at the door of Ebenezer.

18

Sermon Commentary and an Altar Call

T HE CHURCH OFFICE was a lively place, especially on Monday mornings after the worship service. There was a lot for Lillian and Sarah to talk about and lots for me to listen to. Sometimes I listened from my small office, but sometimes I couldn't resist pulling up a chair next to them and joining in the commentary. Somehow they could find the funny side of things, and frequently, it seemed to me, they would find me the center of their jokes.

In the service on Sunday, Daddy King talked about a man who asked him for a ten-dollar loan. "Bless you for having ten dollars," the man had said.

Daddy King paused. "Now, isn't it silly? It would be smarter of me to keep the ten dollars and remain blessed than to give it away. Now wouldn't it?"

Everyone in the congregation laughed, but perhaps I laughed the hardest; something in that story really touched my funny bone. Suddenly he changed the subject to sin and judgment and became very serious. Still caught up in the humor of his story, however, I couldn't conceal my laughter. Cutting off his thought midsentence, he turned to me. "What are you laughing at, Brewster?"

"Laughing at your story," I blurted out. I must have blushed as red as a stoplight.

"From where I sat, I could see you blushing right through the back of your head," Lillian said, bursting into laughter. "Oh, honey child."

Sitting in the choir behind the pulpit, the back of my head was about all that she could see of me, but she called it right. Daddy King went on developing his ideas of sin and judgment as if nothing happened, while I waited anxiously in front of everyone for my blush to fade.

Lillian then mentioned the funeral sermon Daddy King had preached for Sister Suzy several days before. "He began preaching about brotherhood and race relations," she said, "right in the middle of her funeral, about a drinking fountain labeled 'white' that galled him. He went over and took a drink and the police grabbed him and escorted him out of the building. Now what this had to do with Sister Suzy and her funeral, I don't know." Sarah laughed.

"Sarah," said Lillian, "you should have seen that man after he finished the sermon, when Brewster got up to pray. He was sitting with Sister Suzy's family with his head down. When Brewster began to pray, that man looked up, his red eyes opened wide, his mouth flew open, and he looked as if Jesus was standing right there. I thought he was going to get up and run for the nearest exit." They laughed and laughed, with Sarah beating her desk with her hands and stamping her feet in laughter.

"But then," Lillian went on, "you should have heard Brewster's prayer. Brewster prayed for God's mercy and eternal rest as if he knew all about her. What would Sister Suzy have thought of this?" They laughed and laughed.

"Years ago," Lillian went on, after I had drawn my chair a little closer, "Rev preached the funeral of a man he said was going to hell. He didn't hold back, and that hurt the family real bad. Let me tell you, when my mother died — she was an alcoholic, you know, poor soul, rest easy — I told Rev not to mention anything like that. She never went to church, although she belonged here. She was found dead in an alley. So I told him I knew her weaknesses better than anyone, but I didn't want to hear any talk about where she was going. 'Oh, no. Nothing like that,' he said. 'Let's get this straight right now, before the service,' I told him, just to make sure. Well, Rev heard me, too. He preached a good funeral.

"During his sermons he's liable to do anything. People are used to that. Sometimes he calls me and I come down from the choir. Like the other day in church. He called me and I came on down to the edge of the choir. Then he whispered something in my ear that I didn't hear. I had to bend way over." She stood up and then bent over, sticking her backside way out and giving it a shake. Then she straightened up and danced around the room as she and Sarah laughed and laughed. "Bless his heart. I don't even know what he said and it didn't seem to matter."

Lillian grew pensive as she continued. "Sometimes in his sermons he says more than he wanted to about someone. 'Did I say that?' he asks me afterward. 'I couldn't have said that.' He'd do anything for anybody, day or night. Do you remember, Sarah, him preaching the funeral of the woman who sold whiskey?"

"My, oh my," Sarah exclaimed. "She used to take her truck and drive up to her brother's shed. He had a still back in the woods and they said he made a pretty good mixture. She loaded her truck full and drove off. Now, she came to church and everyone knew what she was doing. Some people complained. We never knew who she sold it to but we had some pretty good ideas. Nobody ever let on that they bought it. Rev talked all about her life when he preached her funeral and you can imagine where he thought she was going. People kind of nodded their heads, but I think a lot of folks missed her when she was gone."

One Sunday was especially dramatic for me, though I noticed that Lillian and Sarah didn't react as strongly as I did.

Toward the end of his sermon, which he titled, "Misplaced Emphasis," Daddy King paused. It was a long pause, uncharacteristically long, in which it seemed as if he were looking each person in the congregation right in the eye.

"If anybody in this church doesn't try to be a Christian, get out," he cried out in a voice like thunder. "I don't want him here." He paused. "How many visitors are here?" About fifty people raised their hands. "How many non-Christians are here?" he asked. One man sheepishly raised his hand, looking around to see if any others had raised their hands along with him.

Leaning heavily on his pulpit, Daddy King addressed that man, whose hand seemed frozen in the air. The congregation was tense, wondering what would happen next. But Daddy King's voice was low and gentle when he next spoke. "Brother, thank you. You are a young and fine-looking man. You don't belong to any church?" The man, looking terrified, shook his head, slowly lowering his arm.

There was another long pause as Daddy King looked out over the congregation, which looked nervously back and forth between the man and Daddy King. "Mrs. McCullough," he finally said, addressing a large woman sitting several pews in front of the man. "Please sit next to our guest and talk to him." She was the head of a prayer group and a deep-river kind of believer. She stood up, went right over to the man, and sitting down in a seat made vacant for her, began talking to him.

Daddy King, addressing the congregation, talked about God, Jesus, brotherhood, and how we need each other. While he went on at some length about joining the church, I watched Mrs. McCullough talking to this man. As Daddy King was speaking, Mrs. McCullough knelt down to pray. Over Daddy King's gentle voice, I could hear the soft voice of Mrs. McCullough quietly praying with this stranger.

Presently the organist began to play a hymn, and I could see that many in the congregation had closed their eyes and bowed their heads. Slowly the man rose to his feet and came forward.

"Welcome, brother," Daddy King said, as he shook his hand. The head deacon came to him, welcomed him warmly, and led him out of the sanctuary. Soon another man and then a woman came forward, and they in turn were welcomed and led out of the sanctuary.

A woman who had raised her hand as a guest remained seated. A deacon had been sitting next to her, talking quietly. Daddy King urged her to come forward, but she refused. No one could move her. Then a middle-aged woman walked down the aisle, and as she neared the podium she flung herself toward the pulpit, onto the floor, and began weeping. An elderly woman sitting there quickly knelt beside her, gently patting her on the back and praying until she became quiet.

I could hear the sobs around the church slowly growing louder as Daddy King talked above the organ playing hymns in the background. Daddy King waited for someone else to rise. When no one came forward, he quietly signaled to the organist to begin the hymn. Soon everyone was standing and singing together one of the great old hymns of the church.

"Rev can sure bring them in," Sarah commented.

"Now, when Dr. King preached for a few weeks in a row, not many people joined. Nowadays," Lillian added, "preachers are all philosophers. When I was a girl, preachers could preach and bring the people in. Daddy King got impatient because people weren't joining his church, so he conducted a revival and brought in six people that day."

"Yes, Lord," Sarah said in response.

"Thank you, Jesus," Lillian echoed, emphasizing each word slowly, until she came to rest on "Jesus" with almost a shout. "We've got a church in Ebenezer. Thank you, Jesus."

19

Brother,
Are You Saved?

I HAD BEEN VISITING my friends Esther and Bill Turner in the country. Since they had an evening engagement, I headed back to Atlanta about mid-afternoon. A few miles down the road I began to see signs advertising a revival. This is where one could find salvation, some signs read, while others boasted of the best quartet singing to be found in the area. On a whim, I veered off the highway onto a small country road and followed the signs that pointed to the revival. I had never attended a revival before, but I had heard much about them from Daddy King. Curiosity led me into this unfamiliar world of country revivals with white people.

I was not alone. Several cars, driving slowly, preceded me, and others followed. Their speed was unusually slow, so I wondered whether they were as eager for salvation as the signs said they should be. "Salvation Is Yours, Now," several signs read, but it was clear that we proceeded along the road not as if we were late for a ball game. Being late for salvation is another matter, I thought.

Then another sign came up. "It's Never Too Late," it read, timed well on the road to address our trepidation and our remorse. I could feel something in me hesitating, like the drivers in the other cars. A tent housing the promise of salvation should not be the same as a tent housing a few elephants and a clown. I suspected, however, that for those eager for entertainment, both served more or less equally well as distractions from the routine of daily cares.

I parked my car in a newly mowed hayfield beside the looming white tent and settled into a seat near the back row. A male quartet dressed in bright blue suits and matching shoes was singing gospel music, accompanied by a pianist who was also dressed in bright blue. Having sung bass in octets in both high school and college, I was eager to listen, especially to the bass. He was tall and thin, and when he hit and held a low C, I was impressed. This quartet was soon followed by another, this time dressed in bright red suits with matching shoes, and then by another dressed in purple. I was enthralled by this singing, so unlike the Episcopal and Presbyterian choirs with which I was familiar. I was so taken by the music that I forgot about the salvation part of this tent meeting until the preacher, wearing a black robe, slowly walked up to the microphone carrying a large black Bible in both hands and singing "Shall We Gather at the River?"

There were songs, readings, and prayers. "Before the evening is over," the preacher said, "many sinners will be purified. You will be freed from the devil and be saved. Hallelujah."

Then he asked, "Are you sitting next to a sinner?" He paused, giving the congregation a chance to look around. "Look at your neighbor," he said. "Your neighbor in the chair beside you is sitting next to a sinner," he declared. I looked at my nearest neighbor and he looked at me.

"I guess I'm sitting next to a sinner," he said.

"I guess I am, too," I replied.

"All right," the preacher went on, "all you sinners come forward into the arms of Jesus. He will wipe away all your sins."

The tent was only about half full with people fairly well spread out, so he urged everyone, every sinner, to come forward, to gather around as a family, to taste the sweet savors of salvation. At his strong urging, people rose and began to move forward. Suddenly I began to feel scared, and as I saw many people standing and taking new seats in front, I slipped out into the parking lot. People were still driving in and parking their cars, so I felt unnoticed as I drove out.

I thought that if they had seen me leaving they would surely say, "There goes a real sinner, Satan-possessed and lost to God, going down into the fiery pit to mess around in the den of vipers. Save him, Jesus, from eternal damnation." At that moment, however, salvation was my little Chevy, carrying me down the road and far away.

I had to admit, after a few miles, that part of me wished I had stayed and seen the meeting through to its end. Perhaps I had lost courage when the preacher asked all the sinners to come forward into a tight family. Crowding in so close to these fellow sinners made me want to burst out of the gates and get free. But part of me wished I had taken the risk and, as one sinner crowded in and rubbing shoulders with the next, taken what came as part of my initiation into rural America's encounter with revival preaching and the salvation trail.

Mulling over my regret, I remembered another revival meeting that was taking place very near Ebenezer. I had sometimes heard their music and singing when I occasionally left the church late. When I asked Lillian about this group, she told me not to pay attention to such things.

"Lordy, Lord, they're a bunch of Holy Rollers. I heard they had snakes in there, poisonous snakes, and if they bite you and you die, they say the snake bit the damned and let the saved go free." I asked her if it was safe for me to go there. "Sure, honey, it's safe," she said. "But why would you want to go there? Ebenezer might never see you again if you get bitten by one of those snakes. I wouldn't, if I were you."

But all Lillian had done was arouse my curiosity. Still sorry that I had not remained in the tent meeting, I kept my car pointing toward the other revival near Ebenezer. As I parked, I could hear loud singing accompanied by tambourines. It suddenly occurred to me that everyone in the tent meeting had been white, but that now if I went in, I would be the only white person. I lingered in my car with my window down, listening to the music and watching the people sitting on their porches or on the steps, just hanging out in the heat of the summer evening. Many were tapping their feet in time with the gospel music, beer in hand, heads swaying back and forth. Occasionally a group of children would run past, involved in some game. Hearing the singing "Lord, Lift Me Up" and feeling its power, I said to myself, "Okay, I'll do it."

All at once I found myself going down a staircase and into a dark basement. Two women in white gloves and white hats with black dresses greeted me, without a hint of surprise. They led me into a room filled with people. The only lights in the room shone on the pulpit and on a picture of Jesus kneeling in prayer. The room was so dark that at first I couldn't see where I was going. They placed me on the aisle, near the back, and then left.

In front, near the pulpit, a group of six people — four women and two men — led the singing. The women were beating tambourines and the men were clapping, all improvising elaborately on the music. I loved the music, but all at once it hit me. What was I doing here? As my eyes finally adjusted to the dark, I saw that I was the only white person in the room. I observed people turning around and whispering.

Because this was now a matter of personal courage for me, I was determined to stay until it was time to leave, unless the snakes really were let out of their cages and sent slithering toward me in the dark. I would draw the line at being tested by snakes. I could imagine the snakes would be happy to find me in the company of the damned and would give me a bite as one of their own.

Perhaps this time I was in deep water, way over my head. In spite of my display of raw courage, I was terrified. I began making plans for escape. Perhaps when everyone was standing, singing with their eyes closed, clapping, even distracted by ecstatic screaming, I could slip out, almost unnoticed in the darkness.

As I was making all these plans, a warm hand touched the back of my neck, then a second hand rested on my shoulder. Startled, I looked up and saw a woman behind me. She was so dark that I could not see her features, but I noticed that people in the chairs behind me had made room for her to stand squarely at my back. I sat there without moving. Her hands also did not move, but simply rested firmly on my neck and shoulders.

The choir became quiet, a few people who were standing sat down, and the preacher stood up and walked to the pulpit. I could hear the chair behind me moving and could feel the hands of the woman shifting slightly as she knelt down behind me and began to pray.

The preacher began his sermon by talking about snakes and vipers, being saved from the snake pit of hell and from the viper's den of damnation. Jesus will save you. Repent. Repent. Repent. The people shouted back, Amen. Amen and hallelujah. Behind me, the woman kept praying in words I couldn't understand, punctuated only occasionally by "Thank you, Jesus."

While the preacher was calling out, Repent, repent, the woman whispered in my ear, "Are you saved, brother? Has God saved you from the fires of hell? Are you saved into the arms of Jesus?"

No one had ever asked me that question. I wanted to get up and run out the door, but her hands pressed so firmly on my shoulders that I was unable to move. "Are you saved?" she kept asking. "Tonight you can be saved."

I didn't know what to say. I couldn't simply say yes, and
certainly I didn't want to say no, but I felt I had to answer
something. Finally, I muttered, "I think so," nodding my head.
I didn't want the preacher and the congregation to turn on
me and force me to the altar.

"Do you know if you are saved?" she asked again. How
could I really say yes? I questioned the idea of people claim-
ing that they had been saved, as if they knew the mind of God.
That wasn't my type of Christianity. They didn't ask that question at Union Seminary or in the Episcopal churches where
I felt at home. Now I was pinned to the screen, the way a
luna moth fluttering toward the light is nabbed by a collector.
Was I now in the grasp of some bounty hunter out hunting for
converts, or was this just some stranger's warm hand trying to
welcome me into a foreign land?

I couldn't get up and leave and I couldn't say yes or no. I
just sat in front of her, listening to the preacher calling sinners
to repent and hearing her ask whether I had been saved. "If
you don't know, you haven't been saved. What you need is
Jesus."

The choir began quietly to sing and steadily grew louder
and louder. I could feel them working into a great crescendo;
then all four tambourines began to shake and crash. All at
once, two men somewhere behind me began to beat wooden
boxes with their canes in agitated syncopation. I wanted to
turn around to see but I was riveted to my chair by two mysterious hands, and it was too dark to see anyway. People began
shouting. Several people stood up and cried, others jumped
up and down, and still others fell over and were caught by
people next to them, who brought them gently to the floor.

Then the preacher began walking slowly down the aisle into
the congregation. He paused every few feet, grabbing people
by their heads and shouting, "Are you saved?" Those who
shook their heads received a prayer, resounding throughout

the room over the din of the singing and drumming. "Are you going to hell?" he asked, pulling them up onto their feet. "Do you want to go to heaven?"

"Yes," I could hear people say.

"Do you accept Jesus as your savior?"

"Yes, yes, please."

"Hallelujah," he shouted while they fell back as if unconscious, buoyed up in the arms of the people near them.

I was sure he was coming for me. The music was at its highest intensity, the congregation was singing, the tambourines were crashing in syncopated rhythms, and the two men were beating on the boxes at their feet, when suddenly the preacher turned to face me. He clasped my head so hard that I thought my skull would break. "Brother, are you saved?" he shouted over the music and all the commotion, looking right into my eyes. "Are you saved, brother?" he asked again.

I was paralyzed, not knowing what to say as he waited for me to answer, when all at once, before I could say anything, the woman behind me, with her fiery hands pressing on my shoulders, shouted back, "He is saved, Reverend."

"Are you sure?" he shouted, gripping me even harder and peering into my eyes.

"He is saved, Reverend," the woman answered back.

"Hallelujah. Thank you, Jesus. Hallelujah, hallelujah," he shouted. "You are washed clean forever in the blood of the Lamb." He grasped my head between his viselike hands in one final squeeze, and as he shouted his final hallelujah he released me. I fell back as he suddenly moved to the other side of the aisle.

The woman's head was still close to my ear, her hands still pressing on my shoulders, and I turned slightly toward her and whispered quietly, "Thank you."

"Thank you, Jesus," she said. "Glory, hallelujah. Thank you, Jesus."

"Thank you," I whispered back again, hoping that she had really heard me.

For the first time in that place, I relaxed in my seat, listening to the music, watching the people, and even singing myself. Slowly the preacher moved forward toward the pulpit and back into the light. People were still working over one another; some who had lain prostrate on the floor began to sit up, others who had been swaying violently back and forth began to slow down, and others who had been praying and weeping became quiet. I was amazed at their energy as well as at their gentleness.

How long I watched this, I do not know, but as I took in this amazing experience I soon noticed that the hands had left my shoulders. I turned slightly to look and saw that the woman had gone. When did she leave me? I turned all the way around looking for her, but she had vanished into the darkness. The space where she had been was once again filled with people. I felt bereft. I sat there, my eyes filling with tears.

Was I saved? That question came around to haunt me again. What does this mean? I kept wondering. My head spun with questions. How can anyone claim to know the ways of God? How can anyone be so confident as to say, "In spite of all my sins, I have been saved?" or to answer yes or no when the question is sharply put. Salvation of this sort is not how salvation was supposed to appear on the well-planned journey of my faith.

But I still felt the places where the woman's hands burned with white-hot energy into my shoulders and down, down into my body. My skin still felt on fire from the fire in her palms and fingers. The preacher's words still resounded in my ears, "Are you sure?"

And still resounding were her blessed words, coming out of the darkness, calming the seas of terror: "He is saved, Reverend."

Was I saved? That is a complicated question for me. If I think too much about it I still am caught somewhere between the eternal yes and the eternal no of life. One thing I do know, however, is that when I entered those deep and terrifying waters that night, suddenly, like the ancient miracle, the Red Sea parted and I was guided by mysterious hands to safety on the opposite shore.

20

Invitation
to the Conference

IN THE MIDDLE of July, I heard about a Quiet Day with a focus on nonviolence, sponsored by Quaker House, and I decided to go. Richard Gregg, who had written *The Power of Nonviolence*, was the day's leader. Having worked with Gandhi in India, he possessed both a profound historical understanding of the effectiveness of nonviolence in the struggle for freedom and a spiritual conviction and compelling depth. I sensed that here was a deep well, and I was grateful to be in his presence. His quiet respect for the human race held up to everyone the vast resources of the human spirit. He said that spiritual discipline was as important for the Christian as physical discipline was to the athlete. But we neglect this discipline, he said. In fact, we know very little about what it might mean for us.

After his talk the people in attendance, who were all white, argued for nearly an hour about whether spanking was appropriate in child rearing. I felt frustrated that the audience seemed to have missed the point after he had spent the day causing us to reflect on nonviolence as it related to our own spiritual development and to the freedom movement right at hand. Sure, spanking was an issue, but the oppression of black people right at our doorstep was crying for attention. I was the youngest person there; I just couldn't bring myself to lead the

group into the deeper and more troubling waters of race relations and the civil rights movement. "A cold spring has a
firm bottom," Gregg had said. I knew I was in the presence
of someone who was standing firmly on the spiritual ground
I admired. I just let that discussion go, aware that I had been
touched by his commitment to nonviolence and his sincerity
and depth in the face of struggle.

Over lunch I met two Presbyterian ministers from the same
congregation, who said they were leading their congregation
in a series on Christian ethics and race relations. I wondered
where they stood on these issues and whether they had a
youth group that was involved in them as well. I asked if we
could meet in their church in a few days to continue this
discussion, which they seemed happy to do.

In a few days I found myself in their office, anticipating a
good conversation and much-needed support for my proposed
conference with youth groups from around Atlanta. The head
minister began by remarking that they had at least one vocal
segregationist in their church, and probably more, who kept
asking why Negroes wanted to be near white people. The
segregationist wanted blacks to want to be near blacks and
not to want to come into white neighborhoods.

"What did you answer him?" I asked.

"I didn't know the answer," he said.

I gulped. "They only want to be treated like human beings,"
I said. "Like anybody else, they want to enjoy the rights due to
anyone. That doesn't mean that they want to be *near* anyone.
Just to be where they choose to be, like you and me."

"That's interesting," he replied. "I hadn't thought of it quite
like that."

I asked if he had a youth group and when he said yes I
offered to bring some young people from Ebenezer to meet
with them.

"I don't think they are prepared," he said pensively. Then turning to his assistant, he asked, "Do you?"

"No," the assistant said obediently. "No, they are not prepared for this just yet."

"Well, I could prepare them," I answered quickly, feeling frustrated by the direction this conversation had taken. "Nothing happens if nobody starts," I said, perhaps a bit sharply. Immediately I was ashamed of my sudden anger, after listening to Richard Gregg talk about nonviolence just a few days before. Finally I broke the silence. "When does your youth group meet next?" I asked.

"Next Sunday evening."

"I will come over and bring several of our young people to meet with your youth group."

He sat there not knowing what to say. Eventually he replied, "I'm not sure I'd know what to do."

"I could find two students and lead an interesting discussion."

He thought a minute. To my great surprise, he then agreed. "Can you find two students who would mix well with our students?"

I knew what he was asking, but I simply said, "Sure, that's easy."

I was eager to make final plans for the conference that I had set up featuring Dr. King, but I was still lacking white participants. I now had a date at the end of July — only two weeks to assemble the participants. I spent the next few days on the phone. I called about ten churches, and this time I found four or five of them receptive. Cautious, but receptive. When possible, I tried to visit the clergy to ease their fears and to establish my legitimacy and the value of the conference.

A few days later I was walking into an Episcopal church. The minister and a woman in charge of church programming met me and led me into their office. Their warmth suggested to me that I would have a better reception than I'd had at the other churches I had visited. They listened while I told them what I was doing at Ebenezer and what I had planned for the conference. They laughed easily and seemed to encourage me to talk on. Finally I stopped.

"What do you think?" I asked.

The minister was quiet for a moment and then asked, "What are the ontological repercussions which will ensue from this conference or whatever you call it? What would happen when you are gone and we have to live with it? How many police are you having? There will be police, of course. What will you do about the reporters who will be there? Do you want them? If they mention a name in a bad context, that person will be socially dead. What are the speakers speaking about?"

For a moment I was speechless. All I could think of were his words "ontological repercussions." I almost burst out laughing, but I held myself back. Those were new words in the context of the resistance to the movement. And the statement that some people might be socially dead if their names got out caught my ear. While these thoughts raced through my mind, he spoke again.

"What are the speakers talking about?" he asked. I told them Dr. King would be speaking, and several others. "It's a bit late to be fuzzy about this, isn't it?" he asked. The woman had been taking notes during this conversation. When I became more specific her pen took down all my words.

"Are you requiring any credentials?" he asked.

"No," I replied.

"That's fascinating." He paused a moment, then continued with his cross-examination. "Separate but equal — what's wrong with that as long as it's equal?"

"Well," I said, and then I paused. Poor man, I said to myself. Poor man. I will answer all these silly questions if you feel you need to know the answers before you do anything. "Separate but equal," I said, "is never equal. The real issue is not about racial equality; it's about equal opportunity, equality of opportunity." I had read the Supreme Court decision *Brown v. the Board of Education,* and he sensed that I knew my position well. He didn't answer me but kept returning instead to the effects the conference might have on the lives of parents and children.

"If there is any possibility of negative consequences, it is best not to do it," he said.

"Yes," his assistant agreed. "Where seeds of danger exist, it is better not to water them."

"It's worth a try," I replied, attempting to be positive, even though I felt that I was quickly losing ground.

"But I see the possibility of grave repercussions which might jeopardize individuals in the church. Yes, we must be aware of these."

I was beginning to feel paralyzed by this circular conversation. "I think the possibilities for good outweigh the possibilities of harm," I said, wanting to end this discussion and get away as fast as possible.

I felt like a foreigner in this church — out in the open, in no-man's-land, where I sensed they were trying to throw a net of fear over my head to paralyze me just as they were paralyzed. I could see this fear in their eyes and feel it in their questions. I began to feel sad for them because they were so stuck. My hopes had met the solid wall of their fear. And I wanted to leave immediately.

What is it like to fear social justice so much that one is held back from doing what is right? How does it feel not to have the courage to do what you quietly believe God is fighting for? I began to sense that my courage was beginning to be put to the test.

Near the end of this conversation I could hear Daddy King's words when I had complained about hitting dead ends and facing real discouragement. "Pick yourself up, Brewster," he had told me, out of experience far larger and more painful than mine, the experience of being hurled to the ground and being rejected again and again. "Don't let them stop you. Pick yourself up, Brewster."

I ended the conversation by again extending the invitation. "This will be an exciting conference. I hope I will see you there." I wanted to say that I knew the ontological repercussions that would ensue from the conference would be extraordinary, but I held my tongue.

"We will want to talk it over with the parents," he said, and after some congenial parting words, I left.

I spent the next few days with several members of the Ebenezer Youth Organization, visiting as many places as we could in Atlanta that concerned themselves with civil rights. Ronald, Eddy, and Charles went with me on this extensive research tour. We visited and spoke with people at the Southern Regional Council; the Episcopal Society for Cultural and Racial Unity; Oasis, a moderate group growing out of Help Our Public Education; Quaker House; and SCLC. These organizations had stacks of excellent material on all the important issues of the day, including voting; schooling; the psychological aspects of integration and segregation; sociological reports on integration patterns around the country; prejudice, fear, and myths related to these problems; and of course, the role of churches within the movement. We picked up armloads of this material and brought it back for our reading and for the Ebenezer library.

As the EYO members discussed this literature, I found them starving for knowledge of the issues and desperately wanting engagement in solid conversation about them. I was trying to prepare them for this upcoming experience, in which I might pair them with white students in small-group discussions.

In the course of this day Ronald told me he had applied to a white high school in the previous year. He passed the first rigorous test — receiving the highest score among the fifty black and white students who were competing. He had high hopes for a good education, but with the third battery of tests he was rejected. Ronald was as smart as any young man I had known, and I was most distressed when I heard this. No one who knew him could imagine why he would have been rejected. Nothing more was said about his experience. It just hung there like countless other experiences that reminded the whole church where people in the white system stood.

Several days later I brought two of our members to visit the youth group at the Presbyterian church, whose minister I had visited. Somehow I missed the exit to the church and drove twenty-five miles before we realized my mistake. After reversing our way, we arrived about an hour late. I was deeply embarrassed. I was afraid they would hold our lateness against the students, reinforcing their stereotypes about black people being slow and tardy. But it was my mistake. After we arrived, however, we entered right into our discussion, and nothing was said about it.

"Dr. King spoke in Jackson last night," one white girl said. "I heard it on the news."

"What did he say?" I asked. I had heard the same news myself, but I wanted her to speak about it.

"He said freedom is coming. There is nothing anyone can do about it. Freedom is coming."

With that, the discussion heated right up, spurred on by two members of the white group who seemed especially antagonistic to Dr. King. While other white students criticized their views, I kept asking them questions to draw their positions out. Soon I asked the two EYO youths to speak about the

Atlanta sit-ins. They described the events in highly dramatic terms, as they had helped organize the sit-ins and move them forward. When they discussed their time in jail, the white group was enthralled. At the end of the meeting I issued the invitation to the Ebenezer Conference. They lunged at the opportunity.

"Can we bring our friends?" several asked.

"Yes," I said, "your friends would be more than welcome."

Then I asked the two who had been most antagonistic to us, "Will you come?" They looked at each other and shook their heads.

"Oh, Charlie," one girl pleaded. "Come on."

"Jimmy," said another girl, "please come with us." But they stood together and shook their heads.

21

At Home with the Kings

THE ELECTRIC ICE CREAM FREEZER was an important gadget in Daddy King's household. To say that he liked ice cream with a few peaches tossed in would be a great understatement. Frequently during the hot summer, I would be asked to fetch the freezer from the basement closet and load it up with ice and salt while Mrs. King poured in the mixture she had prepared. "He will be home soon, and he likes his ice cream," she would say. Then we would set the freezer on the edge of the patio and I would start cranking, tending it with ice and salt as necessary. I had to be careful because a few weeks earlier I had made a mistake and somehow let the salt water rise over the lower lip of the lid and spoil the treasured mixture.

Daddy King came home about 9:30 one hot night, and when he heard the freezer grinding, a big smile broke out on his face. Mrs. King and I lifted the container carefully out of the ice water and brought it over to the sink to wipe it off. Then we delicately lifted off the lid to see if the ice cream was hard enough and to taste whether any salt had crept into it. She always kept a large oval platter nearby on which to lay the dasher. When I made a slight move toward the dasher, she beckoned me away, reminding me that the dasher was always reserved for Daddy King. He stood nearby with a large bowl, at which point Mrs. King backed away and watched with delight as he plunged his spoon into the ice cream, loading his bowl with a generous heap mixed well with peaches.

"When I eat cream, I eat cream," he said, as he moved toward his favorite chair.

Just as we turned on the TV, Coretta called on the telephone to ask Mrs. King where she might take her children to have their tonsils removed. Suddenly, Dr. King appeared on the screen. "He's on the news," Mrs. King told Coretta in a perfectly natural voice, as if she were describing an everyday occurrence in the home. She hung up the phone and returned to her seat to watch.

Dr. King had been speaking in Jackson. "Freedom is coming," he said.

"Yes it is," replied Daddy King, talking to his son as if he were in the chair right next to him. "Boy, they hate that," he said in a strong voice. "They'd like to get at him, but they can't because he's right. They can't say anything because he is right," he said looking back at me. "He gets white people mad because he wins people. He can't help winning. He has won people over since he was a boy."

"Segregation is dead," Dr. King went on. "The only question is how expensive will they make the funeral." We all had a good laugh at this, carefully holding our bowls of ice cream so they wouldn't spill. Daddy King shook his head, looking at me as if to say, "that's the talk of greatness." I nodded, indicating a strong yes. Daddy King then became quiet, musing over the TV image that had quickly come and so quickly gone.

I had noticed that the dasher had been left in the bowl, but I wasn't going to touch it, tempting as that was, even though it was melting away. After his second bowl, Daddy King walked over and picked up the dasher and cleaned that off well. It was obvious to me that he had been waiting for this all along. "Very fine. Very fine," he said.

During the course of the summer, one day blended into another as I comfortably settled into the routine of the Kings' family life. Occasionally something unusual would happen, however, that would dramatically break the course of the normal day's events. On one occasion, the Kings had a guest who visited them for about a week. About forty years old, she had known the Kings for a long time from her work in southern churches. She was given the room just up the hall from my bedroom.

The first night that she was there was unusually hot, and I slept with little on. Sometime around 3:30 my door opened and I became aware that someone was in my room, moving quietly toward my bed. All at once the other houseguest flopped herself down right on top of me — and then let out the biggest scream I had ever heard. She jumped up, still screaming.

Soon the light appeared in the hall. The light revealed that my visitor did not have much on either. Bathed now in light, I dove under the sheets as Reverend and Mrs. King charged into my room.

"What's happening?" he asked, dodging out of the way as their nearly naked guest ran down the hall to her room and slammed the door. Daddy King looked at me and then at Mrs. King, waiting for some explanation.

"She seems to have fallen into my bed by mistake," I muttered, not knowing what to say. He looked at me in amazement, and then at Mrs. King, and then at the guest's door, standing there bewildered, just shaking his head.

"Well, get your sleep now, Brewster," he said.

"You too," I said. "Good night."

"My gracious," I heard him exclaiming as he turned off the hall light and went back to his room. "Good Lord."

It wasn't easy to get to sleep after that because I kept wondering what breakfast would be like when the guest appeared.

Breakfast did come, finally, and the guest came downstairs and greeted me as if nothing had happened. Perhaps she thought that I had slept peacefully through all the commotion and would not remember it in the morning. I chose not to mention it, and we chatted amiably about Tappy chasing squirrels or some other conversation fillers until Mrs. King came down the hall with Reverend King. We all greeted each other and then loaded our plates with the breakfast I had prepared.

"Well," Mrs. King began, "that was quite a night wasn't it?"

"I hope you got some sleep," Daddy King added, looking at us both with a twinkle in his eye. It was clear to me that their guest didn't want the incident mentioned at all, but Mrs. King went right on.

"Reminds me," she said, "of another time long ago. Remember, King?"

"That's enough, Bunch," he said, half seriously, half joking.

"We had a houseguest."

"Bunch, you don't need to tell them about that," he said, getting more serious and somewhat agitated, but Mrs. King went on, undeterred.

"We had a houseguest, and one night this man was in the bathroom, sitting down, you know." She didn't say it was Daddy King, but it was very clear to us who the story was about. "All the lights were off and the house was dark as pitch. Suddenly he heard footsteps in the hall and the bathroom door opened. This nameless man just sat there, so scared he didn't move. He didn't know what to do, when suddenly this woman turned, pulled up her nightie, and sat right down on his lap. I have never heard such a fit of hollering in my life."

Daddy King and I burst out with great laughs, until we noticed that the guest didn't even crack a smile. She saw no humor in Mrs. King's story at all, and Mrs. King, still laughing but sensing her discomfort, tactfully changed topics.

Several times during the summer, the whole family came over for a barbecue: Christine, the oldest child, with Isaac Farris, her husband; Dr. King and Coretta and their children; and Dr. King's brother, A. D., with his wife, Naomi, and their children. It was a large gathering with lively talk and energetic play by the children. Many people attended to the cooking, both grilling the barbecue outside and preparing everything else inside. As usual we needed ice cream, so I was put in charge of the freezers. We would sometimes have three freezers going at once, driven by their electric motors, while I enjoyed the old freezer I had cranked by hand, letting the children take turns keeping the handle turning. I promised them the reward of licking the dashers if they continued, and I had no end of volunteers.

Sometimes I would go up into my room just to let the family be together, even though they assured me my presence was no intrusion. One evening as I was preparing for bed, I heard a knock on the door. It was Dr. King. "How about a little peach cream, Brewster, before you go to bed?" he said as he handed me a heaping bowl.

"Thank you, thank you," I said.

"Now, you have a good night," he called out as he left.

"And you, too," I replied.

22

Soul Food

MY FRIENDS took great pleasure in introducing me to good, old-fashioned southern cooking. "Now this is real food," they would say, "real soul food." I liked to eat and I liked to cook, so I was a welcome candidate for one family or group after another to try to outdo the last in presenting me with "real food." Sometimes they would offer a special creation along with the other food on the table and not say anything until I tasted it. At other times there would be a fanfare, and I would be given a special presentation to try before the others had moved their forks. And at still other times I could sense a snicker welling up from somewhere. As I raised my fork to my mouth the conversation would stop, and all eyes would look at me with great anticipation to see how I would react.

Sometimes just for fun, while sensing this little joke, I would rest my fork on the unknown serving and then after a pause, dig robustly into the mashed potatoes or beans. Eyes would silently meet and the conversation would resume, until I moved my fork toward the special serving again.

Obtaining the recipes was no easy matter. When I asked how to make Hoppin' John, for example, the typical response would be, "Oh, a little of this and a little of that, until it tastes just right."

"What spices did you use?" I found myself asking repeatedly. Pointing to a spice, the cook would say, "Oh, a dash of this, perhaps a little more, more or less. You add it until it tastes real good. Then let it simmer until it blends real nice."

Of course, people had different opinions as to how to cook their favorite recipes. "My mother always said to do it this way," one cook would declare, but another cook's mother always did it another way. And then there were men who cooked, some of whom discovered new recipes and some of whom followed a mother or father or some other relative who was a recognized expert around the stove.

I always felt a sense of accomplishment when I finally obtained a recipe that I could use. Take Hoppin' John, for example.

HOPPIN' JOHN

6 cups water	1 bell pepper
1 teaspoon cumin	1 teaspoon chili powder
1 pound black-eyed peas	1 onion
1 teaspoon thyme	2 cups uncooked rice
1 cup bacon	6 cloves garlic
1 (6-ounce) can tomato paste	Salt and pepper to taste

Cook the peas for 1 hour. Brown the bacon, add the green pepper, onion, garlic, cumin, and thyme. Add tomato paste, chili powder, water, and beans, and add the rice. Make sure there is about 1½ inches of water over the top. Cook covered, about 30 minutes.

Oh, no, another said. You never mix the rice and beans in the pot. You mix them on your plate. My mother always told me that's how it's done. Now, honey, here's how you do it:

2½ pounds black-eyed peas	1 or 2 onions
Ham hock or salt pork	2 cups rice
½ teaspoon red pepper	1 cup diced celery
2 bay leaves	Garlic, salt, and pepper to taste
2 tablespoons diced bell pepper	

Soak your peas overnight. Cover ham with water and cook. Then put in peas and other ingredients and water to cover the peas. Simmer 2 hours until they are tender, not all broken up. Serve alongside rice, with collards and cracklin' bread. You can use corn bread if you prefer.

"Collard greens?" I asked.

COLLARD GREENS

1 ham hock	1 cup vinegar
½ teaspoons red pepper	1 small onion
4 pounds greens chopped up	1 teaspoon sugar
into bite-sized pieces	Salt and pepper to taste

Simmer for 45 minutes to 1 hour, and there you have it.

And cracklin' bread? "Some cracklin' bread is mighty good with this."

CRACKLIN' BREAD

½ cup salt pork or bacon	2 cups corn meal
1 teaspoon baking powder	1 cup water

Sauté salt pork or bacon and add it to the mixture of the other ingredients. Put the mixture into a skillet in the oven and bake at 450°. You can make this as one cake or small little cakes.

"This makes for mighty fine eatin'."

"Someone told me that you make Daddy King's breakfast," another said. "Try this some time and see what he says. My family calls this Johnny Grits."

JOHNNY GRITS

1 pound sausage	1 clove garlic
2 eggs	1 to 2 cups grated cheddar
1 cup grits	Cayenne pepper to taste
½ cup milk	½ cup butter
4 cups water	2 tablespoons Parmesan for the top

Cook the sausage and crumble it. Cook grits and stir in the cheddar, eggs, butter, milk, garlic, and sausage. Pour into a baking dish, sprinkling the Parmesan nicely over the top, and bake 40 minutes to 1 hour at 350 degrees, until nicely browned.

"I have something special this morning, Reverend King," I said a few days later. I had gotten up early and put this all together and started it cooking an hour before breakfast.

"Well, well. What do we have here?" he asked as he came down the stairs. "Bunch," he called out. "Look at this. What do you call this?" he asked.

"This is Johnny Grits." I told him confidently.

"What in the name of heaven is Johnny Grits?" he asked. "Let me try some." He took a bite. "Mighty fine," he said. "Hey, Brewster, you're quite a cook."

I thought everyone would know this dish as Johnny Grits, but perhaps only the family that gave me the recipe knew this name. I'll call it Johnny Grits, and I would agree with Daddy King — mighty fine it is.

At picnics, a lot of commotion was made over a fine potato salad. There were several cooks known for their salads, and when they came with a heavy bowl or platter, people would gather around in anticipation. I could feel the sense of well-being descending over the gathering when a fine potato salad appeared. "Now we can eat," people would say.

Here's one recipe, carefully recited by one of my favorite potato salad cooks. "You come aside and write down what I tell you. And you don't have to tell anybody, either, ya hear?"

Potato Salad

2 pounds potatoes
1 teaspoon celery salt
½ cup chopped celery
1 tablespoon sugar
½ cup chopped onion
1 tablespoon vinegar
2 tablespoons bell pepper
½ cup mayonnaise

⅓ cup mayonnaise
   with the vinegar added
1 hard boiled egg
2 tablespoons celery seed
⅛ teaspoon pepper
7 or 8 sweet pickles
1 teaspoon salt
Paprika

"Now you stick pretty close to this and people will take notice," she said, with a wink of her eye. She was in her seventies, I'd say, tall and thin, with round silver-framed glasses. "I want to tell you something else," she whispered, and with a tap on my elbow, she guided me off the one side where we could have a private conversation. "I work with a family of white folks," she said. "They have a big house, I tell you, lots of rooms, but I have the kitchen. That's my castle. Where I am the boss. You better believe it. What comes out of my castle warms the whole house. When I dress up in my whites, everyone knows the house is a-humming. I have raised a generation of their children, too. I washed them as babies, cradled them in these old arms of mine, I put Band-Aids on their cuts, I wiped away their tears, and I watched them grow up. And I shed a few tears of my own, don't you know? I'm like an old post they all lean on when they need to do a little leaning, from the Mr. and the Mrs. on down. I don't know what they would do without me. I may not be able to rest my tired feet in Rich's Department Store, honey, but I'm the queen of my castle. Now, you go and try my salad, ya hear." As I eased toward the potato salad, I suddenly found my elbow being tugged in earnest. "Come follow me," another woman whispered in my ear, almost dragging me over to another table. "Now these are mine," she said proudly, as other people looked at her with surprise. "Now this one is sautéed okra and that one is gumbo, potluck gumbo. These are from about as far south as you can get. Any farther and you are mixing in with the alligators."

I took a taste of each. "Oh, yes," I said. "How did you make these?"

Sautéed Okra

Take 1 pound of okra, cutting off the stems, and boil for 1 to 2 minutes. Dry, and then slice crosswise. Mix the okra in corn meal, if you like, with salt and pepper, and fry them in butter and garlic for about 5 minutes.

Potluck gumbo was new to me as well. "Here's how you do it," she said loudly enough so that other women could overhear.

POTLUCK GUMBO

¼ pound ham	1 onion
½ cup parsley	4 ounces crab meat
1 pound shrimp	1 green pepper
½ cup scallions	5 cups water
1 pound okra	2 cloves garlic
Salt and pepper to taste	1 tablespoon gumbo filé seasoning

Sauté ham, then shrimp. Boil okra, pepper, onion, scallions, and parsley for 1 hour. Then add ham cubes, shrimp, and crab meat, and cook 15 minutes. The final 5 minutes, add salt and gumbo filé. Serve hot over rice. "Now you can just sit back and enjoy this."

Over the summer, I had corn nuggets, sautéed okra, all kinds of string beans and potluck gumbo, to name a few dishes that were new to me. A lot of my education over the summer came out of the kitchen.

One day I was a little late for dinner, and when I arrived I saw Dr. King's car parked in the driveway. When I got to the table I found the place set for me opposite Dr. King. They seemed especially glad to see me on this occasion and were eager to have me join in a fine dinner. They passed a dish toward me and I scooped out a healthy serving. The table became suddenly silent as they watched me closely.

Dr. King broke the tension with a huge burst of laughter as he watched me looking closely at what was on my plate. "Never had trotters before?" he asked.

"Trotters?" I exclaimed. "No, never had trotters before."

"This is how you eat them," he said as he put some into his mouth. I could see the bone moving around, pressing on one side of his cheek and then on the other, as he sucked out the tender meat. "Fine, fine," he commented with great satisfaction as he spit out the bone. "Now you have one."

"Trotters," I said. "Trotters?"

"Pigs' feet, Brewster," Daddy King interjected, and they burst out laughing. "Bunch cooks them real fine."

They sounded most distasteful to me, but I didn't let on my feelings. I was willing to try anything, and seeing how much Dr. King was enjoying himself as he worked the pigs' feet around in his mouth, and hearing Mrs. King's cooking complimented so favorably by Daddy King, I plunged right in. Yes, they were fine. My technique was a bit rough, good for another laugh all around, but I had to admit they were real fine. "Yes, real fine," I said.

TROTTERS

12 pigs' feet, split in half	2 cloves garlic
10 to 12 peppercorns	4 onions, chopped
4 bay leaves	3 tablespoons salt
4 cups cider vinegar	6 stalks chopped celery
2 teaspoons crushed red pepper flakes	1 tablespoon Tabasco

Scrub the trotters well, put them with all the ingredients in a pot, and cover with cold water. Boil and then simmer for 3 to 4 hours. Then you've got yourself a fine dinner. Real fine.

One evening I was the guest of honor at a family cele-bration. The mood was festive and full of fun as the food was passed around. I was hungry, and I served myself well. I caught sight of a girl about twelve years old looking at me with a wild gleam in her eye. I looked around the table and found they all were looking at me, waiting for me to begin. There was undisguisable mischief written all over their faces. I sensed a joke. What was I getting myself into this time, I wondered.

It smelled so good that I took a big mouthful and suddenly the whole table cheered. "What are you laughing at?" I asked.

"Well," the host asked, "how do you like chitlins?"

"Good gracious," I laughed, "am I eating chitlins?" I paused savoring a mouthful. "This is some fine food," I told them. I had to admit that I was glad I had tasted them before I knew what I was eating. Made out of the small intestine of a pig, their dictionary name was chitterlings, but everyone called them chitlins. My eating them was the cause of much laughter.

"Now Brewster is eating chitlins," they all commented. Just how fast and far the news spread around the church, I don't know, but it traveled like a scandal, because on Sunday the word was out: "Brewster loves chitlins."

CHITLINS

10 pounds chitlins	1 clove garlic
2 teaspoons pepper	1 tablespoon Tabasco sauce
1 onion	1 bay leaf
¼ cup vinegar	1 tablespoon salt

Wash your chitlins thoroughly, 5 or 6 times, then place all ingredients in a pot. Don't add too much water. Simmer for 2 hours. Remove excess water. Remove the chitlins and cut them into pieces, about 2 to 3 inches long. Continue cooking 2 hours, until tender. Season to taste. Now, this food reaches far back into the souls of people, and it seems that you eat this with a full sense of the history of what has gone before.

A heaping bowl of string beans accompanied the chitlins. String beans were usually cooked with bacon or hog back, and this fat filled the beans with wonderful, rich flavor.

STRING BEANS

5 slices bacon	1 pimento, cubed
2 pounds green beans	1 onion
2 cups water	Salt and pepper to taste

Put bacon in the water and cook for 10 minutes. Add onion and salt. A few minutes later, add your beans. Cook 15 to 18 minutes. Discard bacon. Mix the pimentos into the beans for decoration. "Now, these beans are a fine dish that goes with many things."

When I came in one day, Mrs. King was working up a mixture of peach ice cream. I can think of nothing in the realm of food that made Daddy King happier than a huge bowl of peach cream, as he called it. I fetched the freezer and made sure we had enough ice and salt. Soon I was cranking slowly, listening to the wonderful sound of ice churning around in the wooden pail. Over the summer I had perfected the process — after the notorious mishap when a pinch of salt crept into the mixture and ruined it. I had been embarrassed, knowing that everyone had been watching me and waiting to lick the dasher.

The door flew open and a big smile broadened on Daddy King's face. "Peach cream for dessert," he exclaimed. "I can use that." And was it good, too! Here's how it's done.

Peach Ice Cream

1 quart light cream	*1 pint cream*
10 nice peaches, chopped	*¼ teaspoon salt*
5 eggs, beaten	*2 tablespoons vanilla*
2 tablespoons corn starch	*2 cups sugar*

Blend light cream and beaten eggs with corn starch, salt, sugar, and cream. Cook slowly until it drips off the spoon, about 15 minutes. Add in the vanilla and peaches. Chill for about 2 hours. Pour into the freezer and start cranking — and keep cranking until your arms get tired and the mixture hardens.

The main course was ended, the table cleared in preparation for the grand entrance of the dessert. I carefully lifted out the dasher and placed it on a large platter, tasting it just to make sure. Then I put that in front of Daddy King. "My, oh my. Look at what you've produced," he said, beaming at the thought of digging in. Then all at once, Mrs. King darted back into the kitchen and brought out a chocolate raspberry upside down cake, and placed it in the center of the table. "Now this is eating," Daddy King said. "Where did you get that?"

"I just got it," Mrs. King answered, coyly.

"Now that is some cake," Daddy King exclaimed again. "And with peach cream. Good heavens."

Mrs. King never told us where she found that cake. And I never did get the recipe. The taste, however, lingers on my tongue to this day. And the look of it, with red raspberries floating on top of a dark chocolate cake, is enough to bring out a great, beaming smile, just like Reverend King's smile, that comes from deep within the satisfied soul.

23

Visiting People

S OME OF MY HAPPIEST MOMENTS during the summer came in the afternoons, when I was sipping a cool drink in the shade on someone's porch. It was during the visits to individuals from the church that some of my real education took place. I chose to focus on visiting the elderly and the shut-ins. Lillian and Sarah, after poring over the lists, would guide me toward the people whom they thought would welcome me most warmly. Perhaps they also knew that the people they had me visit would gently open the eyes of this white boy from the North so that he could see a scratch or two beneath the surface of their ordinary life.

I found myself one sweltering afternoon in an old rocking chair opposite an elderly woman in her porch swing. My chair creaked each time I rocked, and the chains of her swing squeaked as she glided back and forth. She handed me a glass of Kool-Aid and picked up her church fan.

"What are you here for?" she asked, not one to mince words. When I told her of my work that summer, she sat without saying a word, rocking back and forth and waving her church fan across her face.

"Well, I still work for a white family at my age," she said. "Been working there for twenty-six years. Oh, they never come here, never seen my house. You are the first white person that has sat himself on my porch. I walk a few blocks, rain or shine, and they pick me up at the corner. I used to take the bus. Now I prefer to be chauffeured, so they pick me up in their car and I rustle into the back seat and look out the window."

She paused for a moment then began again. "I get eight dollars a day, after twenty-six years," she said, pausing to let that number sink in. Then she reached for her purse, tucked in under the folds of her skirt, and pulled out a wrinkled photograph of a white family standing with her in front of a house. It was a large house, and several children were playing happily in the yard.

"It's their summer cottage, a $125,000 cottage," she said, pausing again. She picked up her fan and gave a little push with her feet to start the swing swinging back and forth, all the while looking at me as I sipped my Kool-Aid and gently rocked in my chair.

"That's right," she went on. "I get eight dollars a day and I've worked for twenty-six years, faithfully, seeing children and grandchildren grow up, holding them in my big black arms, cuddlin' them in the nigger lovin' way. I love them, but how can you live on eight dollars a day? How can you retire without a retirement?" She shook her head. "You know, I've found the richer white people are, the stingier they are with their money."

I nodded my head, imagining clearly what that white family must think: She is so loyal and loving. We couldn't get along without her. Twenty-six years is the best part of our lives. We would do anything for her. We are all she has. Eight dollars, you know, isn't too bad, after all.

Yes, they would think that, I said to myself, but how little they know of what she is really thinking when she holds up that photograph of their family and her smiling in front of that large, white house. This family would be surprised if they had seen her at the sit-ins and in the marches. "What do those people want?" they would ask her. And they would have been incredulous if they could have seen her walking in the streets waving her cane and holding a sign that said, "I Want Freedom Now," singing "We Shall Overcome."

Her genius — or was it something else — had enabled her to smile through her job for twenty-six years, because she wonders, Where else can I work for eight dollars a day and be loved by the people I work for?

"I have cleaned every surface in that house and every toilet bowl a million times over, but they have never seen my house or sat in your rocking chair, where you are rocking."

Yes, I would have another glass of Kool-Aid when she offered it, just for the opportunity to rock beside her in her creaky old rocking chair, swinging in her swing as we two passed the time away, rocking and swinging, gentle and easy. I hated to leave, because I knew I was in the presence of an amazing person, but the afternoon passed by and she said her dinnertime was coming around.

A few blocks from Ebenezer was a cotton mill where one of the church members worked. He came by the church frequently. From time to time we'd pick a shady spot and sit down on the steps for a chat. He worked for a dollar and a quarter an hour, managing machines.

"I'm pretty good with my hands, and a pretty good mechanic," he said. "There's white men been on the job less years than I have who get two-fifty an hour for doing what I do," he said.

"Couldn't you organize?" I asked.

"Us Negroes? We're afraid we'd lose our jobs, because we couldn't get new ones," he replied. "The mill fired five men suspected of union talk. One word, even just one suspected word, and I'm out on the streets. At a dollar and a quarter an hour I have one job in the day and one at night. I don't know of a man like me who can make it with just one job. Fifty dollars a week isn't enough to feed, clothe, and house a family. And then send your children to college. I got dreams for my children, just like every other man. You can't just stamp out a dream like you stamp out a cigarette butt."

He got up and paced around and soon returned to the step. I was sure some painful thought had made him restless; he kept shaking his head and mumbling something I couldn't hear. When he sat down he continued.

"Sixteen hours a day, six or seven days a week, with no vacation, year after year, don't create a happy home life. My wife works for five or six dollars a day and our children are turned loose like cattle to forage in the streets with the house locked behind them." He just shook his head. "Very often homes are broken, the father gone somewhere, perhaps with another woman, perhaps the mother is off with another man. Too much liquor. Too much liquor. Poor people reek of alcohol. Poor people, poor people, just drowning their sorrows, because it don't pay to dream." His voice trailed off into a thick, heavy silence.

I was quiet, feeling the intense misery weighing so heavily in this man's life and sensing that behind all this misery was the system white people had created and struggled so hard to maintain. How could he experience all this and not be consumed with bitterness, I wondered. Here and there in this community I had met a number of real saints, who still held on to the hopes of generations and who somehow still turned to God with genuine gratitude in their hearts. Having suffered and struggled beyond my comprehension, they lived with dignity so fragile and with love that could so easily be destroyed by fear or resentment. It seemed strange to me how such purity of spirit, such profound hope, even such abiding gratitude could exist in the midst of deep suffering. Whom had I known in my life who had struggled as much as this man had? Could I have survived his life?

"Now, you have a good afternoon," he said to me, breaking my brief reverie as he got up and turned to leave.

"See you soon," I said, smiling a friendly farewell. I remained sitting on the steps for a few moments in the shade, just watching him walk away down the street.

During the previous few weeks I had come to know a union organizer who attended church regularly. I approached him one day and said I wanted to talk with him. About a week later, he followed up on my request and showed up in the office.

"Why don't you two go upstairs to Rev's office," Lillian suggested. Sitting in the comfortable chairs, I expressed interest in his work in the unions.

"I'm at home in a union meeting," he said. "That is church to me." Like some of the other people I had talked to, he jumped right into his subject. "The people say, 'Well, the boss folks are religious people. They go to church.' Don't ever say that to me. I tell them, Don't ever say that to me again. At $1.25 an hour, if your child gets sick in the middle of the night and has to go to the hospital and you have no money to pay the bill, will your boss roll out of bed and stretch out his hand to help? You say he is religious. At $1.25 an hour, don't even say that to me again. Do you hear me?" He had gotten right into it, and as he sat in Reverend King's office his eyes began to blaze. He stood up, his fists tightened. "Don't ever tell me your boss is a religious man."

Sitting down, he talked more quietly about a woman he had seen that week. "She has a fifteen-cent insurance policy and she is still scrubbing floors at the age of seventy-eight. It is a desperate job, my Lord. She comes to church and her minister asks her to tithe and give all she has, and so she gives to the church what she owes the light company, because she has a dream of going up there afterward. That's the only reason she goes on scrubbing floors and going to church. She hopes her suffering will bring her a reward. That is what keeps her going on and on. Life, you know, is complicated. Sometimes you think you understand something, the truth maybe, and yet it is wrong to tell it. What would you say to this woman? Who knows the right answer?"

After he left, I could still feel his anger hitting me like a baseball bat. Here was a man who could say, "Thank you, Jesus" and yet be filled with outrage at the same time. He had caught hold of the idea that the church could focus people's minds so much on heaven and the hereafter that they had no will to fight for heaven on earth, in the present.

"The church can cripple people," he had said, "make real cripples out of stout-hearted men. It can sweep moral outrage right out of a man's soul. The church can make people so afraid of hell that they'll do anything just to keep from going there. Anything. I mean anything."

I had never really heard such rage joined up and connected to Jesus. And I had read about, but had never seen right in front of me, such outrage against the church for making the heaven of the future so desirable that it could render people who yearned for justice absolutely powerless. I could feel the power of his experience leaning against my theology and pressing it into new channels. I felt somewhat threatened by this because I agreed with him, and yet I did not know how to organize my thoughts to fit what I was experiencing. Where were my high school teachers, my college teachers, and my seminary teachers? Why had all the preachers I had ever heard watered down the teachings of Jesus so much that his moral outrage was lost? Why had I been kept in the dark, and why is this message kept hidden from people?

A few days later I visited a man who lived in a high-rise apartment building. The complex, built with government funds a number of years previously for the elderly poor, was in good condition. The walls looked clean, the screen doors swung easily on their hinges, and the paint was new and clean. I saw people milling around, and suddenly I realized they were all white.

I didn't have an apartment number, so I searched out the main office and inquired. "I'm looking for Mr. Judson's apartment," I said to the person sitting behind the desk.

"You mean the nigger called Judson?" she asked.

"Yes," I said. "But what did you call him?"

She paused for a moment, looking me over. "What you doin' with him?"

I told her what I was doing and she stared at me in disbelief. "You from his church and callin' on the shut-ins. Lordy Lord. What's next? Oh, he's over there," she said, pointing to another building, saying it in an offhand way, as if to dismiss me.

I found the other building and buzzed Mr. Judson. Soon he came downstairs to greet me. "Call me Judson," he said, extending his hand in a warm handshake.

I looked around the building and quickly realized this was the black facility. The paint, instead of being fresh and new, was gray and peeling, and there were no screens on the doors. He said the overhead fan had been broken "for as long as time outta mind."

While he was showing me around, a group of white women came by, touring the building. They had just been across the yard looking at the building for elderly white people. The woman who had given me directions was showing them around. As I stood there with Judson, I noticed that she wanted to guide her little group around us, but since we were standing conspicuously together in the middle of the room, some paused to say hello.

"How beautiful," one said, and the others agreed. "How nice this is," they commented, looking at Judson.

"Come on girls," the woman said, and they all followed her into another room. Judson and I looked at each other. He shook his head.

"Who are they trying to fool?" he asked. "They just don't know." After he showed me around we paused at the elevator. "This is separate but equal," he said with a sneer. "Does it look like separate but equal to you?"

24

Some Mighty Big People

BEFORE I WENT to Atlanta I had been led to believe that Rosa Parks started the modern civil rights movement, in 1955. I imagined this event had important forerunners, but I knew little about them. Every once in a while something would slip into my conversation with Daddy King, such as the struggles of the teachers in the 1940s, the march to City Hall to register in the 1930s, or the recurring confrontations between white businessmen and the black community.

Since he and I frequently had breakfast together, I took the opportunity to ask him questions about his experiences in Atlanta. I was increasingly interested in his work as a civil rights leader because we were now hearing so much about the work of his son. What was becoming clear to me was that Dr. King's work was part of a long family history of leadership in the struggle for freedom.

"When did you begin to work in civil rights?" I asked one morning as we sipped our coffee.

"Where do you want me to start?" he asked, suggesting to me that the subject was so vast that I had better be more selective in my questions. I said that I wanted to start at the beginning. "Oh my," he said, and then turned to look out into his yard at Tappy running around after squirrels.

"I remember one day when I was a young boy," he began. "My mother forgot her lunch." He described how he picked up her paper bag and walked over to where she was working. He climbed the steps of the big house and the front door was wide open. "I saw my mother on her knees scrubbing the floor and the white woman standing over her watching. I stood there and looked at her. When I appeared, offering her the paper bag, she looked shocked. 'Get around to the back door,' she scolded."

Then he described watching his father plowing behind a mule on a white man's land. "To my little head, what my father was doing just didn't seem right. Maybe it all started back there for me," he said wistfully. "Maybe my little spirit began to be a fighter for justice back then. That was a long time ago. I never knew why they hated us so much. Still don't, really," he said.

"You know, Brewster, it all comes around to one word. That word is 'nigger.' There is pain on both sides of that word, for white people and for Negroes. I saw a lot in Stockbridge, and I saw a lot in Atlanta when I finally got here."

"Like what?" I asked.

When he got to Atlanta he worked in the railroad yards. He described seeing white men bossing the blacks around. "I saw these big Negro men smiling back at them. We were all happy darkies, smiling our way through the day. Oh, I smiled too," he said, pausing, "but under the smiles was a fire of resentment just smoldering away." His mouth grew tight and he looked angrily out into the yard. "Separate water fountains, sometimes no fountain at all, and separate bathrooms, and sometimes no bathroom at all. When I saw Negroes walking to the back of the bus or giving up their seats to white folk, I got hot inside. I got hot when I saw Negroes smiling at white folks and white folk smiling back as they took their seats or led Negroes out some back door to a dirty bucket for a toilet." He paused and twisted his mouth up as if he were re-creating a grotesque smile on his face, and then stopped suddenly. "Never do that again."

He came to Ebenezer in 1931. "Over the years I did a lot of hollering. I think people got tired of me hollering so much, but I just couldn't stop. The Negroes kept asking, 'When?' The white folk kept saying, 'Soon.' Behind the 'soon' was the word 'never.' We knew that."

He began to see that voter registration was the key that would unlock the door to freedom. The ballot box. He wanted all the black churches to be the center of a drive for voter registration, a huge mass meeting at City Hall, but the ministers rejected him. " 'Don't rock the boat, King,' they said. 'Don't rock the boat, King.' This is what they kept telling me."

Ebenezer had a history of civil rights work. Before Daddy King came, Reverend Williams, his father-in-law and the minister at Ebenezer, organized the black community to stop a bond issue that made no provision for high school education for blacks in Atlanta. Because of his work four years later the Booker T. Washington High School was opened. "Now that was quite an accomplishment," he said with pride. Reverend Williams was also the leader in establishing the first black YMCA. "Reverend Williams and Ebenezer got results.

"In 1935 I had had enough, enough of don't-rock-the-boatism, enough of 'you're going too fast,' enough of soon, soon, soon, and I organized Ebenezer and the Negro community into a march. Was Atlanta surprised! I told the community, all gathered together, I ain't going to plow behind no more mules. I ain't gonna be pushed around no more. We're marching for freedom now. Been waiting a long time."

"What happened?"

"Well, we marched downtown, right up to City Hall, past angry policemen, past crowds just looking at us, and into the registration office. Two hundred Negroes registered that day. Can you imagine that not one newspaper carried that story — because they didn't want the word to get out about how orderly we were and how successful we were?" He paused for a moment, and then continued. "Nobody gave us anything. That is the sad story of civil rights in America. Everything we got we had to take for ourselves.

"Now, you would have thought," he went on, "that a few white leaders would have come forth. During the 1930s not one white leader would stand up and be counted. Not one in the whole city."

"You must have gotten discouraged," I said.

"Yes. Many people got discouraged. This was the Depression. People without jobs and nowhere to go. Negroes were afraid they wouldn't live long enough to get what they were looking for. Hard times, back then. Real hard. People just don't realize, today, just what we had to go through."

"What did you do after that?"

"You really want to know this history, don't you, Brewster?" he said, laughing.

"Sure. What happened next?"

He then described how, in 1936, he opened his house to the black schoolteachers. A black teacher would teach first grade and get half the pay of the white teacher who taught first grade. They were afraid to strike because they'd all lose their jobs. He realized that they were too vulnerable to lead, so he took on the leadership.

"The school board couldn't get at me when I was in the pulpit. Oh, I got hate mail. The Negroes said I had a big mouth. 'Don't rock the boat, King,' the ministers cried, but I had to go on. Once you start you can't turn back. And I couldn't turn my back on those teachers. That battle took eleven years before Negroes got the same pay as whites for doing the same work with children.

"White people would ask me over and over again, 'What do Negroes want?' What do you say to that, Brewster?" He shook his head in disgust. "What do you say to that?"

Daddy King talked at length about applying economic pressure to the white community to bring about change. The picket line was the best weapon the blacks had to challenge the economy. If blacks weren't served at a lunch counter or were told to endure any number of practices designed to humiliate them, this would be cause to picket and boycott. "Change came slow, but it came, nevertheless."

After World War II, the pace of change increased. Blacks came back from fighting side by side with white soldiers on the front lines in France and Germany and refused to follow the signs saying "Colored" — colored go here, colored go there, colored go to the back. The Supreme Court came out with favorable decisions. By 1947 over twenty thousand blacks had registered in Atlanta. The mayor, William Hartsfield, even tried to force the issue, but he would only go so far. He integrated the police force but he would not allow black policemen to arrest white people.

"Can you imagine that?" Daddy King asked. "It seems funny now," he said, laughing at the absurdity of it. "That's only thirteen or fourteen years ago.

"Meanwhile I was raising my two sons and one daughter. M. L. would ask me, 'Why do white people hate me, Daddy? What did I do to them?' " He shook his head again and wondered. "What does a father teach a son? It tore me up inside. When he was a little boy he asked me that."

He was quiet for a moment, but then as he turned to look outside he began to chuckle.

"What are you laughing at?" I asked him.

"One day I was in the mayor's office, trying to negotiate something, and the mayor just didn't understand the daily humiliation of Negroes. I was getting madder and madder and he finally said something that set me off and I pounded the table so hard with my fist that suddenly that table split. Right there." We laughed and laughed.

"Must have had a lot of power in that fist," I said, laughing.

"Never got anywhere negotiating, but they wouldn't forget that meeting for a while."

Things happened in the 1950s and 1960s, he went on to say. In 1955 Rosa Parks started off the great boycott of Montgomery. "This is what I had been saying all along. Get out the boycott. When their economy collapses they will change. All the talk about soon, soon, soon, stops when that bank account shrinks. Then they finally call us to the table.

"All the time we fought for civil rights in Atlanta there was no white minister who helped us. That hurt. When the white churches could have taken a lead, there was no one with the courage to stand up and be counted. That hurt real bad. Hurt the cause of civil rights, but also hurt the standing of churches and how they deal with blatant injustice.

"Well," he went on, "a new generation was coming up and they saw me as an old man, a thing of the past. They wanted to lead in their own way. The sit-ins in Greensboro came along, and then the sit-ins moved to Atlanta. White people wanted to protect their private rights but Negroes wanted their rights, period. The whites were angry. White businessmen took a hard line. That just fired up the Negroes."

"Do people today remember what you did twenty or thirty years ago?" I asked him.

"Memory is short," he said. "A lot of people think Rosa Parks started the civil rights movement and helped get the sit-ins going in Greensboro. Memory is short. Long before today's leaders were born, people were struggling for justice and suffering for justice. I stand on the shoulders of some mighty big people. Forgotten now, and long gone, but they brought us here. Don't forget that, Brewster. We are here because of some mighty big people."

25

Singing Hymns

FROM THE PRAYER MEETING I attended on the day of my
arrival to the services on Sunday mornings, one of the
aspects of my life at Ebenezer that most amazed me was the
hymn singing. Many of the hymns I had never heard before,
whereas others I had heard once or twice. Just about everything about the way the congregation sang its hymns was new
to me. For instance, at first I couldn't believe how slowly they
sang them. They would linger over the words as if they loved
them so much that they didn't want to let them go and move
on. In my tradition it was as if we loved the words so much
we couldn't wait to get to the next word. And the intensity
with which they sang hymns amazed me. It didn't take me
long, however, to begin to flow with their pace and to appre-
ciate how the words and music reinforced each other as they
inevitably touched the heart.

> Softly and tenderly Jesus is calling,
> Calling for you and for me;
> See, on the portals He's waiting and watching,
> Watching for you and for me.
>
> Come home, come home,
> Ye who are weary come home.
> Earnestly and tenderly Jesus is calling,
> Calling, O sinner, come home.

Such sentiments can only be expressed in the slow pace of the soul's ancient rhythm.

On Sundays, sitting with the choir behind me and the congregation in front of me, I was surrounded by extraordinary intensity. I had never heard such powerful singing. Reverend King loved to sing, and I could hear him above the choir and congregation, calling everyone to sing with all their hearts. And then sometimes the singing would quiet down to a gentle hum, barely heard, forming the ground on which prayers could be sustained.

I also noticed how different the feeling in these hymns was from the ones I loved, such as "The Church's One Foundation," "Praise to the Lord," and "Let All Mortal Flesh Keep Silence." In Ebenezer's hymns, Jesus was a friend, walking and talking, listening and lifting us up before the throne of God.

What a friend we have in Jesus, all our sins and griefs to bear.

This was no distant God praised with intellectual propositions set to good music. Rather, this was the God who walked in the garden in the cool of the evening, searching out the human heart for companionship and for questioning.

What a privilege to carry everything to God in prayer. In these hymns, the relationship to God and to Jesus was the central pivot around which the words and music revolved.

There was another powerful theme that ran through many of the hymns I heard at Ebenezer that was not present in most of the hymns that I had previously sung. People called out to Jesus for help: walk with us, yes, but please save us; listen to us, yes, but please rescue us; salvation is real, yes, but Lord, don't make it so far away that we will never taste it. Though this theme was explicit in some of the words, my ears also picked it up in the overtones of passion and intensity as parishioners called out to Jesus. Have compassion on our suffering, they asked, and lead us out of the bondage we have known so long, into the light of freedom. Give to us a new Exodus; help us to endure the desert; bring us to the Promised Land. In the singing, I felt the impassioned calling out for freedom and justice, mercy and hope, courage and fortitude that would make daily suffering possible to endure so that today would be worth living and the next day would be worth waiting for. This singing reached far back in history and reached forward to that place of coming home.

Being from the North and from the world of white privilege, I was embarrassed at first. The experience about which the congregation sang was not my experience or the experience of the churches that I knew. This was a different world. What a powerful world it was, and I quickly became caught up in it. It was not long before the singing enfolded me. As I grew closer to the people in Ebenezer, I could feel the hymns embrace me with their language, their music, and their passion. Soon I became swept up in seeking the hand of Jesus to hold mine and to lead me on, singing from the heart about longing, thanksgiving, and the abiding companionship of the Spirit.

"How do you like our service?" Daddy King asked me, always curious about how this white, northern Episcopalian reacted to his Baptist worship.

"I love the service," I told him truthfully. "And the hymn singing. I've never heard such wonderful singing of hymns."

"I sang most of these hymns as a boy in Stockbridge," he told me. He described the singing in his boyhood church and how Reverend Low began to call on him for solo singing. He found that he could move the congregation to tears with his singing, and he loved those moments when God seemed close at hand as the people sang out their hopes and longings. "Singing was the best way of keeping people from falling into the abyss of bitterness. Life was hard, and if you didn't sing, how could you hope and struggle?

"I took those hymns right out into the streets when we marched on City Hall," he said. "Singing and protesting go hand in hand. You can't have a movement without singing. Singing and praying and walking. You can't walk far without singing."

I pictured how far this young singer had moved, from singing gospel songs in his rural church and for the revivals when they came by, to leading the singing along Auburn Avenue, in Atlanta, Georgia, accompanied by a large congregation of protesters seeking equal rights. The words of the old hymns were frequently changed so that they fit the needs of the present struggle, but the old hymns were there, giving history, vision, and momentum to the present liberation struggles.

Using hymn singing as the backbone of a struggle for freedom was in my experience not something most Episcopalians, Presbyterians, or Methodists did. In fact, ours seemed to be a religion without struggle. Even though within Union Seminary's walls justice was an important theme, it was justice for someone else or some other group. The idea that my home parish and the parishes in which most of my classmates worked would gather in the streets singing hymns and marching on City Hall was not part of the vision. In spite of the fact that Reinhold Niebuhr, the great twentieth-century theologian, and other great teachers spoke boldly to our classes about justice, I never felt it as my issue. My hymns were not connected with a struggle that would become expressed in the streets and in the courtrooms. They were not created for people to march with arms locked together, moving forward in a great sea of music that reached back generations into history's primal struggles and forward into transcendent visions of redemption.

The congregation was singing "Throw Out the Lifeline" one Wednesday evening as I walked into the weekly prayer meeting. Daddy King was away and I felt conspicuous, like an outsider, being the only white person present. Someone quickly handed me a book and soon I joined in.

> Throw out the lifeline to danger-fraught men,
> Sinking in anguish where you've never been;
> Winds of temptation and billows of woe
> We'll soon hurl them out where dark waters flow.
>
> Soon will the season of rescue be o'er,
> Soon, will they drift to eternity's shore;
> Haste, then, my brother, no time for delay,
> But throw out the lifeline and save them today.

Slowly, as I sang this hymn, deep feelings welled up in me. "Throw out the lifeline to me," I quietly prayed. "Here I am, ready to catch if you will throw." As I prayed in silence, they kept singing, "Throw Out the Lifeline," and I felt they were singing to me: that I was the "danger-fraught man" sinking in anguish where I'd never been.

After finishing the hymn, someone read from the Bible, and then we began to sing "What a Friend We Have in Jesus." While everyone remained seated, singing quietly, one elderly man stood up and swayed back and forth, his eyes shut and his hands folded in prayer against his chest. He began to hum and then to sing, his voice carrying over the small congregation.

> What a friend we have in Jesus, all our sins and griefs
>   to bear.
> What a privilege to carry everything to God in prayer.

As he sang, the congregation began to improvise with the melody and harmony of the hymn, giving him the freedom and support to weave his prayer through the strands of the slow and quiet singing in the room. All at once he began to speak and the congregation shifted into humming.

"I lost my wife, Lord Jesus, and she is gone. Oh, what need-less pain we bear. I am weak and heavy laden, cumbered by my load of care. Precious Savior be my refuge, I will take it to you in prayer."

When he stopped, he began to cry. Several people immediately stood up next to him, singing to him quietly and holding him gently as he swayed back and forth.

"In His arms He'll take and shield thee. Thou shalt find a solace there," we sang, singing both to him and to ourselves, looking to Jesus as a friend to help us carry our sins and griefs. Several people were openly crying, but most of us wept silently, absorbed in our own cares and sorrows. We sang the hymn twice, not wanting to let go of the nourishing vision of the suffering Jesus, our friend, who wanted to accompany this distressed and lonely man on his journey. After the hymn was over, people prayed silently or aloud; others offered words and prayers of support.

All at once, the leader turned to me. "Reverend," he said, "we would like you to say a few words." Then he handed me the Bible.

"How could I?" I asked aloud. "How could I add to what you have just been singing?" I noticed that the people kept on humming, with their heads bowed and their eyes shut, as I spoke those words.

"Not tonight," I began to say, but instead of sitting down, I remained standing as people quietly hummed and waited. "I came here, a stranger. I was afraid. But you threw out the lifeline to me. I caught it."

As people were humming with their heads bowed, I thought they were not listening, but when I said, "I caught it," a loud chorus of "Amen," "Thank you, Jesus," and "Praise the Lord," filled the room. "Now I am walking with you," I continued. "Now we are walking arm in arm. Together we are walking in

compassion and love, for justice and freedom. We have caught
the lifeline and we are walking for our sisters and brothers.

"Thank you, Jesus," I said, and then sat down amid a chorus
of their praises.

"Is there a hymn you would like us to sing?" someone asked.

"Yes," I said, "Blest Be the Tie That Binds." Soon we were
all singing the hymn together.

> Blest be the tie that binds
> Our hearts in Christian love.
> The fellowship of kindred minds
> Is like to that above....
>
> We share each other's woes,
> Our mutual burdens bear;
> Often for each other flows
> A sympathizing tear.
>
> When we asunder part,
> It gives us inward pain,
> But we shall still be joined in heart
> And hope to meet again.

This prayer meeting and the weekly ones that followed
opened my eyes to the way the singing of hymns bound people
together. We became vulnerable, offering our lives to God and
being supported by others who cared deeply. I always left at
the end with the hymns singing in my head and repeating
themselves over and over. The rich resonance of their voices
carried me forward. As I sang them I felt the presence of my
friends who had thrown out the lifeline to me when I was
lonely and out of place and were happy when I caught it.

While visiting some of Ebenezer's shut-ins one sultry afternoon, I called on an elderly man who lived in an apartment
complex. As I left his apartment I saw a woman down the
hall sitting near a balcony on a wooden box, trying to catch

what little breeze there was. I noticed she was singing with her head leaning against the wall and her hands folded in her lap. "I need thee, O I need thee." As she sang her whole body swayed back and forth.

"Hello," I said, as I approached her.

"Who do I have the pleasure of meeting?" she asked. I introduced myself and told her what I was doing for the summer.

"I like your singing," I commented. As she turned toward me, I saw that she was blind and very old.

"I ain't going nowhere, so I ain't in no hurry. I'm only going to Glory Land, but it don't look like it'll be today." She paused a moment. "Can't even see the sunrise," she said. "But then, I can't see the sunset either. Pull up a seat and join my congregation. That'll make two." I saw another wooden box not far away so I brought it and set it down next to her.

"Oh, my, you're a northern white boy," she said, pausing. "And a preacher are you?" I had given one sermon in my life just a few weeks before, the very day that I had arrived at Ebenezer, so I guess I could call myself a preacher.

"Yes, I'm a preacher," I said, suddenly realizing that I had never given myself that title before. "Yes, I'm a preacher. Keep singing," I encouraged.

"Are you comfortable in your pew?" she asked with a chuckle, and then she began to sing "I Need Thee Every Hour." She finished a few lines and then stopped. "I'm blind," she said.

"Yes," I replied. "How long have you been blind?"

"You wouldn't want to hear," she said.

"Tell me," I said.

"I was born six years to the day after President Lincoln was shot. When I was a little girl I saw the most awfulest sight in all my life." She paused a moment as if to gather herself together for the next thought. "I saw my Uncle Jonah get lynched. From a tree, it was. After that I started to lose my seeing. God didn't want this little sweet girl to see anymore suffering like what I saw that day. God slowly closed my eyes, opened my heart, and blessed my soul."

I was quiet after that. Soon she began to sing as if I weren't there.

> I need thee, O I need thee;
> Every hour I need thee;
> O bless me now, my Savior,
> I come to thee.

She sang this three times and then stopped. Her slow, deep singing brought the pressure of God down upon our little congregation. I could say nothing. Finally she broke the silence. "Reverend," she asked, "have you ever gone hungry?"

I was startled by her question. "No, never gone hungry," I replied.

She slowly nodded her head as if to work with my statement. "Ever been kicked off the land with a gun to your head and no place to go?"

"No," I answered. This was followed by another silence, a shorter silence this time.

"You ever slept in the woods in the cold rain because white folks burnt your house down?"

"No," I answered again.

"Ever wanted to run away to safety but had no place to run to?"

"No."

She reached out and grabbed my knee, and facing into my face she blurted out, "What then, honey, do you have to sing about?"

I could say nothing. I felt the chasm between us growing deeper and deeper with each question she asked and with each no that I uttered. I knew there were a thousand other questions that she could ask that would continue to reveal the extraordinary difference between us. What *did* I have to sing about?

My father had gone through real poverty when his father died, and he had to leave high school to support his mother and aunt. But he was a successful lawyer when he married my mother, and he had proudly passed on his new prosperity to his family. My mother had become a pediatrician and spent much of her life practicing medicine with the poor.

I was part of the privileged white class from the North. I knew that, and with each question that I was asked, the gulf between this woman and me seemed to grow wider. I knew little of the experiences of which she spoke. Would this chasm be so broad and deep that we couldn't reach across to each other as two human beings? I didn't know, because the question she asked me I couldn't answer: "What then, honey, do you have to sing about?"

Her hand still held my knee firmly, and her blind eyes soon turned away from my face and upward toward the heavens. We sat in silence.

Presently I felt the early rumblings of another hymn from deep in her chest. She cleared her throat, but instead of singing she began to talk, as if to herself. "Always wondered what white folk sing about," she said. "No slavery; can't sing about freedom. No hunger; can't sing about the Lord's banquet. Never driven from your home; can't sing about the Promised Land. Never had no cross burning in your yard, no lynchings in your family; can't sing about deliverance. Always wondered what white folks sing about. I guess when you're on top there's no place to go but down. They sing about bein' across the river on the other shore." Her voice dropped off into a nearly inaudible whisper. "But they left some of us behind. How do you sing about that?"

She sat in silence for a few moments, looking far away, as if she were looking over at the distant shore, and then, clearing her throat and leaning her head against the yellow wall, she began to sing,

> Into my heart, into my heart,
> Come into my heart, Lord Jesus.

All at once she stopped and squeezed my knee. "I thought we were a congregation of two," she said. "Into my heart," she began again, and this time I joined in.

> Come in today, come in to stay;
> Come into my heart, Lord Jesus.

She began to hum and I hummed along with her. At first I felt awkward singing and humming this hymn so slowly, and in a public corridor with this elderly woman, but her fingers grasping my knee like an eagle's talons, and the open, direct way she sang, finally swept my embarrassment aside. As I began to relax into the hymn, I could feel the power of her deep faith. The great chasm between us seemed to melt away. I quietly placed my hand on top of hers and hummed on, swaying gently back and forth in harmony with her swaying. Suddenly she stopped humming and began to talk again.

"Once I was going nowhere, but with Jesus in my heart, I'm going somewhere. So I sing the sorrow songs of my people that my mammy taught me. Sorrow songs keep me from dipping into the well of bitterness and tasting too much of the sorrow of my people." With her right hand, she clenched her fist and beat on her chest.

> Come in today, come in to stay;
> Come into my heart, Lord Jesus.

"Do you ever sing the sorrow songs of your people?" she asked. My mind raced back to the seminary chapel hymns and the hymns I sang in the parishes I attended. I couldn't think of hymns like that.

"Do you ever sing hymns of the struggles of your people?" The struggles of my people? She must have felt in the silence my pulling back, because again I couldn't answer. What were the struggles of my people? Suddenly she clenched her fist and beat her chest over her heart.

"Keep Jesus in your heart," she said as if she could read my heart. "Call him back in," she told me. "If he's there, you'll find struggles enough. But they'll be his struggles. Lean on him when you get into people's sorrow. Then you have something to sing about."

Then she became quiet and began to work herself into another hymn, "Leaning on the Everlasting Arms." This time she shook me into singing along with her "congregation of two."

> What a fellowship, what a joy divine,
> Leaning on the everlasting arms;
> What a blessedness, what a peace is mine,
> Leaning on the everlasting arms.
>
> Leaning, leaning, safe and secure from all alarms;
> Leaning, leaning, leaning on the everlasting arms.

This time we leaned into each as we swayed to the right and to the left.

"A congregation of two," she said, reaching out both hands for me to take. "Oh, what blessed power in a congregation of two people singing. Thank you, Jesus," she said, beginning to pray. "Thank you for coming into our hearts. Thank you for having arms big enough for both of us to lean on. Now, bless this preacher, Lord. Thank you, Jesus." Then she was silent. Our worship was over.

I got up, taking my time over a gentle farewell.

"Keep singing the Lord's song in this foreign land," she said.

I turned and walked down the corridor and down the staircase and got into my car. I sat there for some minutes, amazed and overwhelmed by my experience and by this extraordinary woman who had lived so long and had seen so much. I knew I would not see her again before she went to Glory Land. She had given me the huge gift of experiencing once again that when two or three sing hymns together, bridges can be built over the great divides that separate people. As I rolled my window down, I saw her approach the balcony. She leaned far out over the railing and called, "Take down your harp from the tree, honey, and sing."

26

My Second Meeting
with Dr. King

THE EBENEZER CONFERENCE that I had been planning with the youth groups was coming up soon. I wanted to talk with Dr. King about the arrangements for it and what I wanted him to do. When he next came into Ebenezer I asked if I could meet with him.

"Who is coming?" he asked me when we were sitting together in his office. I had definite positive responses from five churches, several in the maybe range, and several others had turned us down. He thought for a minute.

"These are suburban churches, aren't they?"

"Yes," I replied.

"What do they think of you?" he asked, rocking back in his chair and laughing.

"Oh, I think they think I'm a radical, a subversive Christian. Someone even called me a communist."

"How did that strike you?"

"I never thought of myself as much of a radical on the outside," I said. "I can look pretty tame. But on the inside, that's different. I'm something of a subversive."

"Here you are in Ebenezer. That speaks for itself," he said. "These people represent a larger system. That system guides them."

"I had not been thinking in terms of systems," I said. "Rather, I tend to think of individuals and of the freedom of the individual to act responsibly."

"Changing individuals is one thing," he said, "but changing systems and cultures is something else. In Montgomery we were up against a system and a culture which perpetuated injustice, up against systemic evil."

"How do you change a system?" I asked.

"By expressing the truth for all to see. By living the truth and not living a lie. By bringing massive economic pressure against it. When you go out to the suburbs with Ebenezer's youth group you are expressing the truth."

He liked the idea of my being a subversive Christian. "You see what needs to be done and you do it. Sometimes the truth is ugly. Sometimes they want to get rid of you because of what you are bringing into the light."

"That's why they crucified Jesus," I commented. "He brought truth into the light. I have the sense that the white churches are curious, but they don't want too much truth. Just a little sniff of truth."

"The church is the great hider of truth," he said. "Eleven o'clock on a Sunday morning is the most segregated hour of the week. Now you're being subversive all right, if you set your mind to change that."

"Me, a subversive Christian," I mused. I hadn't been taught much about how to be subversive. It seemed that the institutions around me were teaching me to support the status quo and to celebrate things as they are. They were training me to be a success inside the system. I saw now that the system in which I aspired to succeed was being labeled unjust. In the eyes of the poor black it was evil. Schools, colleges, or seminaries are not interested in seeing this truth or our country would be a different place.

In Dr. King's presence the idea of being a subversive Christian excited me, but I wondered what it would be like back home. "This can be a lonely road," I said.

"People don't understand you," he replied. "The prophets talk of the few who can save the remnant. I'm going to preach about this on Sunday. I'm thinking about it now. The title is something like 'The Hope of the World Is in a Creative Minority.'

"What are you going to be like when you get back?" he asked. "Part of the creative minority, I hope."

I took some moments thinking about this. Sensing my dilemma, he said, "It's easy to follow along with the majority. Jesus didn't go along for the ride. The Gospels are clear about this. But, oh my, Christianity can make the black look like white. Segregationists quote the Bible all the time. People get confused. Now that you have seen what you have seen, how are you going to fit in?"

A visitor interrupted us, and as Dr. King left the office I sat deep in thought. My world was so different. I could hardly tell anyone here what it was really like at home, and I could hardly tell anyone at home what it was really like here. I was educated to fit in, and yet I didn't fit in. Swirling around in my head was the statement made by my mother's friend who told her that because I was going to work with Dr. King I would never be a bishop. I had never aspired to being a bishop, but now I realized that there might be some truth in that statement after all. Maybe in my heart I was becoming too radical for the church. Maybe I would have to compromise myself too much. Maybe her friend knew I would be changed and would come back such a different person with a dusting of subversion in my soul that I would never fit into the system.

This brief meeting led me to the edge of despair. How was I going to both fit in and change things? I didn't feel as if I could speak with enough prophetic power to change very much in the world. I hadn't been outstanding as a student. As a speaker I was too shy, and as a writer I had no confidence. If I tried to fit in, I imagined that I would always be restless inside, with a world of thoughts and feelings burning in my heart that I found impossible to express. Who was I really, and where was I to go with my life?

Down the hall I could hear scraps of conversation. "Challenge economic injustice," Dr. King said with passionate emphasis, but then his voice sank too low for me to hear.

This thought made me think in another direction about myself. Here I was, by anyone's standard a part of the wealthy class in a world in which economic injustice was everywhere, yet I could not see the cause-and-effect relationship between one person's wealth and another person's poverty. They seemed to live in two different and distinct worlds not linked by cause and effect. The fact that my father had a well-paying job had never been presented to me as an ethical issue. He had struggled to get there. He remained a hero in my eyes. Having enough money and being a compassionate human being were the values on which I was nurtured, and they seemed good to me.

Dr. King soon returned, seeming somewhat agitated. "Economic injustice," he mused, as he sat down again.

"What about economic injustice?" I asked.

"The issue is racism, but it is also deeper than racism. The issue is economic injustice. The rich get rich on the backs of the poor."

"How is that?" I asked, searching for the cause-and-effect link that I couldn't see.

"The cotton fields," he said looking at me intensely. "The cotton fields," he repeated, waiting for me to make the connection.

"The masters got rich from the labor of the slaves," I said.

"And the rich get rich from the labor of the poor," he quickly added.

"The rich need to keep the poor people poor in order to stay rich," I said. He nodded. "I have not been brought up to see the connection," I said, "and nothing in my education has helped me analyze this. It is as if we were blind to this cause-and-effect link that connects the rich and poor. You mention the slaves, and in that example it is obvious, but the connection fogs over in our modern world."

"It is easier for a camel" — the phone rang. "Excuse me," he said, reaching for the receiver, but just before picking it up he looked at me and said, "Jesus made the connection."

I stepped out of the room, my head swirling from this conversation. What was the connection between the people on the Upper East Side of Manhattan, I wondered, and the people who lived in the slums, twenty blocks to the north. Why was the all-important link between the poor and the wealthy so carefully hidden from the wealthy so that being wealthy was not a matter of public or private conscience? How different, really, was the world of Wall Street and Harlem from the world of the plantation and the cotton field? Why was it so hard to see the connections in one and so easy to see the connections in the other?

"Action for justice has to be grounded in philosophical and theological reasoning," Dr. King had said. "Resistance to moral injustice has to come from deep inner conviction." We had talked about Reinhold Niebuhr and Gandhi and their influence on him when his thoughts were taking shape during the Montgomery resistance movement. I realized that the great struggle for justice needed to come from a deep place in one's heart, and I wondered if I was prepared. Perhaps I was still too much on the outside of the movement. Perhaps something was missing in my faith. I felt unprepared for sustained "subversive" action. How could I argue the case of nonviolence? How could I speak with the passion and skill of Niebuhr and Gandhi? I did not feel intellectually or emotionally prepared. I realized that I needed something, but I didn't know what it was. Part of me was afraid to find out. I was afraid to be put to the test. Maybe I would find out during the training session in Alabama in a few weeks. I looked forward to that event, but I deeply dreaded it at the same time.

I heard Dr. King hang up the phone, so I returned to his office and picked up the conversation where we left off.

"You were talking about the old camel," I reminded him, "the camel we toss off as exotic, too exotic a piece of scripture for us to pay much attention to."

"That's the point," he said. "We blind ourselves to that part of Jesus' words that have to do with money." He paused, and I could see his mind was going in another direction. "The hope of the world is in a creative minority. That's my sermon for Sunday. You are part of that creative minority."

"What do people need to get there?" I wondered.

"Faith in God and commitment to justice," he replied as he took out his pad and wrote something down. I sensed that our meeting had come to an end and that it was time for me to go. "Are you coming to Alabama?" he asked.

"Sure am," I replied.

"Fine," he said, "fine."

"Thank you," I said. "And I'm looking forward to your sermon."

I walked down the hall toward the staircase with his last words ringing in my ears. Faith in God and commitment to justice. Did I have that faith, I wondered, and was I really committed to justice, to economic justice? I suddenly thought that racial justice was the easier issue. Economic justice was the real stumbling block.

I greeted Lillian and Sarah and slipped into my little office to think and to take some notes. It seemed as if I had been systematically trained not to see the economic issues, the ethical issues surrounding poverty and prosperity. I had taken a college course in economics, but never was economics discussed as an ethical issue. In those courses, the plantation was one thing, but Wall Street was another. According to the rules, the Protestant ethic, I was allowed to acquire as much wealth as I could, and by whatever means, and it was up to the poor to do the same, to pull themselves up by their own bootstraps. I was trained to make my system work for me, and the best way to do that was to blot out any causal factors that linked the wealth of a few with the poverty of the many.

This understanding extended into the world; our country got rich on the backs of other countries that either got poorer or were kept poor for our country's economic benefit. Why did people not see that the poor countries are simply the cotton fields for the United States and the other rich nations? Why were these questions not being asked in our universities and in our governments?

What an effective system, I thought. It does just what it is supposed to do for the wealthy and the rich. It blots out any sense of mutual responsibility. It allows people to do horrendous things and to feel no anguish, because they never see the effects of their actions, down the line. It allows white institutions to condone countless lynching expeditions — or nowadays, to keep poor people poor or to fight wars and kill people far from home — without feeling any guilt. Our educational system was, apparently, incapable of and unwilling to raise ethical issues, even about its own way of teaching, because, of course, if we are blind to issues, we have no responsibility for fixing them. Dr. King had opened a door that I knew I had to enter. He was trying to teach me to see.

27

"The Promised Land"

WITH THE LONG-ANTICIPATED CONFERENCE just a few days off, I called a final preparatory session of the Ebenezer Youth Organization. More than twenty-five members showed up, bringing phonograph records, refreshments, and the hum and buzz of teenage eagerness. First we decided on our schedule for the next several weeks, to include picnicking, a social, a bowling party, and baseball for the boys and skating for the girls. When I spoke of the importance of the conference, the group went quiet.

"There was a bombing yesterday on my block," one of the boys said. "A dog was killed. No one was hurt. I used to play with that dog. I loved him."

"Who would do a thing like that?" another asked.

Every four weeks or so bombs had gone off during the night in the black neighborhoods around town. The police were called in, but no arrests were ever made. A low level of fear hung over us like smog over a city. No one ever knew the whens or the wheres, but everyone knew that sooner or later a fire or an explosion would tear a quiet street apart and set off a new frenzy of fear and resentment. The whys were known but seldom talked about.

Hearing this, I stood stunned for a moment, not knowing what to say. I was focused on the groups of white visitors, soon to arrive, and was aware that my young people must have been thinking what I was thinking: Could it have been one of them? Could it have been their fathers or cousins or someone they knew?

Then someone caught me off guard with a question in an upbeat tone of voice. "Okay, what are we going to do at the conference? Let's make sure that we give them a great time."

My mind was still churning with rage at the thought of the bombings, but they seemed to have already moved past that. I had never heard of a bomb being thrown in the neighborhood where I grew up, but they had grown up assuming that white people threw bombs randomly, here and there, to threaten and harass the poor sections of Atlanta.

Nevertheless, the group was eager to get on with planning the details of the conference. We would have a welcoming committee, a refreshment committee, and a panel of four who would tell their stories about participating in the sit-ins and being thrown in jail. Then we would have one-on-one discussions with members of the white youth groups before Dr. King arrived to speak.

To prepare for this, we broke up into pairs and told our stories to each other. The question I asked them to address was, Have you ever experienced discrimination and what did it feel like? I urged them to express their feelings; I thought few white youths had ever talked on that level with their black counterparts. Then the phonograph records were pored over, the music was turned on, refreshments were set out, and the party began.

The day of the conference finally arrived, and I was nervous, hoping that after all the planning, all the phone calls, and all the interviews that it would go well. One by one the visitors' cars pulled into our parking lot and were met by our greeters. I stayed inside and watched from a window. The church whose minister had wanted police protection came with several parents, without the minister, while no one came from the church that had wanted to record the proceedings.

Five different churches — three Episcopal, one Presbyterian, and one Methodist — brought their youth groups, bringing the total to over forty youths and seven or eight adults. No ministers showed up. Twenty-five members of the EYO came.

The meeting progressed just as planned. The four panelists talked and answered questions about their experiences in the sit-in movement and in jail. One by one they described what it was like to be refused service at a lunch counter, to be hauled away by police for just sitting quietly, and then to spend time in jail.

"What would you do if the owner refused to serve you because of the color of your skin?" one panelist asked.

"I would punch him out," came the quick reply. Several boys nodded their heads. "Like that," he said, standing up and throwing a punch into the air.

"We are committed to nonviolence," the panelist slowly replied.

A poignant moment of silence followed. "Isn't that the soft way? Isn't it the way of — " he stopped abruptly.

The panelist spoke deliberately, finishing the boy's sentence for him, "The way of sissies?" The panelist shook his head. "It is the way of moral truth. It is the way of higher ethical ground. It is the way of Gandhi and the way of Jesus." The white student didn't know what to say.

I had trained one panelist to ask questions as well as to give answers, and I quietly waited to see what would happen. "Have you ever had your back to the wall and chosen to act according to the highest moral ground — according to the ways of Jesus?" the panelist asked. There was silence. "Have you ever had your back against the wall?" the panelist asked the boy again, who was now shifting his eyes and looking around the room nervously. "What did you do?"

A parent broke the tension. "Nonviolence is an interesting approach," he said, and made a few comments about nonviolent strategies. The white community quickly joined in. I realized that this discussion was taking us off course, so after a few more comments I announced our next event, a one-on-one or small-group discussion. I divided the group so as to place one Ebenezer person with one or two of the white youths, with no two members of a particular white youth group in the same triad.

"Describe an experience in your life," I said, "in which you felt you were discriminated against, and what did that feel like?" After a great rattling of metal chairs, the room was soon filled with the noise of twenty-five small groups of young people talking excitedly with one another. I walked around listening in and encouraging them. In nearly every group my EYO members were talking while the others were listening with full concentration. I had done some rearranging of the groups that had naturally formed, because I wanted to make sure that Ronald, the EYO president, was sitting with the boy who wanted to punch people out. I knew that Ronald could handle himself well and would raise powerful questions with the aggressive boy.

"I needed a drink but I couldn't find a soda fountain that would serve me."

"I needed a bathroom, and all we found through the door in back that says 'Negroes Only' was a bucket."

"I wanted to date a white boy but his parents, when they saw me, wouldn't allow it."

"I was with my father and some white men called him Sambo."

"They called me Nigger Boy."

The room grew very quiet as I heard the youths describing their experiences and their feelings. "They really called you that?" a white girl asked in surprise.

"No, I have never felt discrimination because of my skin color," a white boy said.

"Oh, really. Never? I can hardly believe that."

"Yes, it's true."

"I can't imagine what that would be like. Wow."

Finally I broke up this process and brought the group into a large circle. "What was that like?" I asked. "What did you learn?"

"The person I talked to had never known discrimination," one of the EYO members said.

"I never knew it was so bad," commented a white girl.

"I have never talked to a Negro my age like that before," said another white student. I could see the heads of the other white teens nodding in agreement.

"I never knew a white person could care about how I felt," an EYO member said.

All at once I heard the door open behind me and in walked Dr. King. The room suddenly focused on him as he moved around welcoming everyone with handshakes. When he had met everyone I gathered the group back together and invited him to speak about the Montgomery movement and what he saw to be the work ahead. After he gave an account of the bus boycott, he paused and thought a moment. I could feel a sermon coming on.

"You are the light of the world," he said. "Christians are the light of the world. But too many Christians are taillights and too few are headlights. Now which do you want to be?" Everyone laughed. After a brief discussion, he said farewell and left the room.

We then broke into small groups as our refreshment committee passed out refreshments, and with music providing the background, the reception began. Soon several groups said they had to leave. Before they left, I gathered everyone into a large circle. "Link your arms," I told them. I paused for a moment, giving everyone a chance to look around the room, before we began to sing "We Shall Overcome."

We'll walk hand in hand. . . .

We shall walk in love. . . .

We will walk in peace.

We sang, and on and on it went as people added verse after verse. No one wanted to break up the moment. Finally the music died down and the circle fell apart like pearls from a broken string.

There were cordial good-byes and many thank yous, and suddenly everyone was gone and the church was empty.

I was deeply moved. I was full of pride in my EYO group. What a marvelous job they had done. I went back into my office and collapsed in my chair. I was exhilarated at how the conference had gone but was filled with sadness when I realized how much effort it took simply to bring these beautiful people together. I couldn't imagine this gathering ever being repeated, even after I saw how eager they were to meet again. And I was filled with anger at the system that kept these young people apart and kept prejudice alive.

My quiet moment was interrupted by Grimes, the custodian. "White folks just swarming around here, Rev," he said. "Hard to believe all these people talking so nice together. It looked like the Promised Land to me."

"Thank you, Grimes," I said. "Yes, today the Promised Land was here in Ebenezer."

28

Learning Comes Hard

WEEKS PASSED BY, and in late July the day for the non-violent training conference finally came. I was picked up at the church by my friend Bill, who had taken me to the pre-conference event a few days before. He brought two of his friends, and soon we were on the way to Alabama. My easygoing mood was soon broken by the stares of three white men in a passing car. The car stayed right beside us for several miles, swerving menacingly close.

"You nigger lover!" they shouted at me through the open window.

"Keep calm," Bill advised. I looked away. The pressure of the honking cars behind them soon pushed the other car forward, and after driving in front of us for several miles they finally moved out of sight. I realized immediately that by riding with three black men I had put the others and myself in danger. Angry men in drive-by shootings had murdered white civil rights workers. The congenial atmosphere in the car suddenly turned to fear. From then on I shielded my face from passing cars with a magazine.

I began to wonder what I was getting into. Is this where I wanted to be? I realized that the Freedom Rides, which had come into Alabama only two months before, had been met with the violence of an angry mob that torched a bus and beat many of the riders. I had been sheltered in Ebenezer and by Daddy King, and now I felt exposed, driving into a racial clash. I was terrified.

I walked into a room containing about eighty people, and glancing quickly around, I realized I was the only white person present. This felt very different from being the only white person present at a Wednesday night prayer meeting; there, people called me "Rev" and looked at me with respect and kindness. In this meeting, I was nobody, and few people even made eye contact with me.

Dr. King greeted us warmly. The tone of the meeting quickly became serious when he described the violence that had accompanied the Freedom Rides, the lunch counter sit-ins, and attempts at voter registration. "This is a training in nonviolent resistance to evil," he said. He talked briefly about Gandhi's practice of nonviolence and about the use of nonviolence in the Montgomery bus boycott. Until this time, even though I thought nonviolence was an interesting theory, I wasn't sure I agreed with it. Wasn't it too passive? Wasn't it only for people who wouldn't fight back? Would it really work against an angry mob with guns and dogs? That wasn't where I wanted to be; in my heart I knew I wasn't committed.

Dr. King, however, brought intensity to the meeting as his voice rose. "We are an oppressed people, and we will bring the oppressive power structure down," he said. "We will return their violence with nonviolence; we will return their hatred with love." People began to cheer, and after waiting for a moment, he sat down.

A young woman came onto the podium and looked out at the gathered people. At first she stood quietly but soon she began swaying from side to side and humming "We Shall Overcome." Her body flowed gracefully and her voice was rich in feeling. Quickly the group joined her.

> We shall overcome,
> We shall overcome,
> We shall overcome some day.
>
> Deep in my heart,
> I do believe,
> We shall overcome some day.

After singing several verses we sat down, and she said, "Chase the fear out of your heart with singing." My body was still buzzing with the singing and my hands were sweaty from clasping the hands of my neighbors. She talked about the role of music in the protest movement and how crucial singing was in the struggle for freedom. "There is no movement without singing," she said, "so sing your hearts out."

We divided the room into two groups of forty people and then we counted off from one to forty. We were told to find the corresponding number in the other group. I was number thirty-seven, but I couldn't find another number thirty-seven in the room. It seemed that no one wanted me as a partner. I began to sweat. All at once I saw a cane waving from across the room and an elderly woman beckoned me.

"Are you number thirty-seven?" I asked hopefully.

"That's me," she replied. "Just call me Miriam. Sit down close to my good ear. That way I can hear you." She was small and thin, and very old, it seemed to me, with silver-rimmed glasses and a deeply wrinkled face. But her eyes were penetrating and her warm smile made me feel comfortable.

"Talk about your struggles," the leader said, "your struggles for freedom."

"Okay," Miriam began immediately. "Tell me about your struggles for freedom." She looked at me with piercing eyes and I began to panic.

"I am afraid," I said almost without thinking.

"You are crippled by fear?" she asked. I nodded. "You can't be free when you are crippled by fear. You can't stand tall when your legs are crippled. You can't fly when your heart is filled with hesitation and fear." I had the sense that this woman saw right into my soul.

"Yes," I said. "I am crippled by fear. The only white person in this room of black people."

"What are you afraid of?" she asked, bending over so that her head came close to mine, and her right ear close to my mouth.

"Afraid I won't be liked; afraid I will be rejected; afraid I will be hurt; afraid that my life won't mean anything."

"Jesus was all of those. My Lord, he was, and he made it through. You just got to get alongside the pain of Jesus and he will carry you. But you got to get him inside. Not just in your head. Your fear has cast out your love. You've got it all backward. Your love has got to cast out your fear. Then you will be free." She sat back.

No one had ever spoken to me like that. Shaking inside, I asked her, "Tell me about your struggles for freedom."

She became very quiet. "My mammy and my pappy," she said and then paused, her eyes filling with tears. One rolled down her cheek, zigzagging its way down her wrinkled face. I knew that if ever I could have gotten inside that tear, I would be a wise man. I watched it slowly inch down until it found the crevice of her lips. I watched her in awe.

"I want freedom now," she whispered, "not in the hereafter." She was very quiet again and I was aware that the room was filled with the noise of a multitude of dialogues. "I want to try to love you, a white man, after all that has happened to me in these ninety-three years. Then I will be free." I looked at her and suddenly her hand reached out and held mine. "After all that white men have done to hurt and harm me."

"Time's up," the leader shouted. I bowed my head and our foreheads touched. Then we drew apart and adjusted our chairs to face the front again.

As Dr. King took the microphone, I felt Miriam's presence beside me. "Bobby Kennedy and I have had a conversation," he said, "and he did not like it when I told him the only way to change the evil in this country is through pressure." He described the vision of many thousands protesting, many thousands filling the jails in a massive, nonviolent assault on a massive, violent, and evil system.

He handed the microphone to another leader, who went over the six principles of nonviolence. I was eager to hear and to talk about these. What really was nonviolence? The speaker went to a blackboard and wrote. "This is a summary," he said, "and you can find these described in the handout."

Principle one. Nonviolence is active, nonviolent resistance to evil. It is a way of life for courageous people. It is aggressive, spiritually, emotionally, and mentally.

Principle two. Nonviolence seeks to win friendship and understanding. The end of nonviolence is reconciliation and redemption and the creation of a beloved community.

Principle three. Nonviolence recognizes that evildoers are also victims. The nonviolent resister seeks to defeat evil and injustice, not people. It is a struggle against an evil system.

Principle four. Nonviolence willingly accepts suffering without retaliation. Nonviolence willingly accepts the consequences of its actions. It recognizes that unearned suffering is redemptive. It has the power to convert the enemy.

Principle five. Nonviolence chooses love instead of hate. It is unending in its ability to forgive in order to restore community and create the beloved community.

Principle six. Nonviolence believes that the universe is on the side of justice. It believes that God is a God of justice and that justice will eventually win.

"We will need to do some powerful singing to get through this next exercise," the song leader said. After several songs, she had us arrange the chairs as if they were the seats in two buses. Some of us were to sit in the rear of the bus, some in front. "Some of you will be asked to move to the rear and you won't want to do that." This was an exercise in being pushed around and either taking it or standing up for one's rights.

People milled around for a few moments until they filled the seats. Two men, previously selected, told some at the front to move to the rear. Several went willingly, others refused. The men lifted and dragged to the back of the bus those who refused. They stood threateningly over one man, who got angry at his treatment.

"You bastard," he said. No one moved as this tension escalated. "Okay, okay," he finally said, getting the point of the rough treatment. Then they asked some people in the back to come forward.

"Next group," the leader called. People were slower this time to fill the seats. "Hey, you," he shouted, pointing to me, "get in front of the bus and sit down." The hostility in his voice alarmed me. I took my seat as the seats behind me filled up. Sitting up front seemed natural to me.

Suddenly one of the large men turned to me and shouted, "Hey, nigger, you don't belong here. Get to the rear of the bus." Before I had a chance to think of what to do, I was picked up and dragged to the rear. "Hey, nigger, you don't belong here," they said.

"You want to fight?" one asked threateningly.

"No," I sputtered. The room fell silent as everyone watched to see what I would do. I sat motionless, afraid to move or say anything.

"Cut," the leader interjected. "Next group."

I got up, feeling humiliated. I had never been told to go to the rear of the bus. I had always felt I could sit any-where, and no one was going to tell me where to sit in public transportation. I went back to an empty chair and sat down.

Two other busloads of people role-played. I felt as if I had been singled out, and I was angry inside. I looked around the room trying to catch someone's sympathetic eye but no one made eye contact with me. I felt as if I didn't exist.

"Lunchtime," the music leader announced. I went over and joined Bill; he seemed to be the only person who would have lunch with me. I wished I could go off to some quiet lunch counter and have a sandwich by myself. It would be so peaceful, looking straight ahead, chatting with a waitress and enjoying a sandwich all alone. There was a Woolworth's just down the street. Then I realized that, yes, I could go there and rest, but not one other person in the room would be able to join me. Bill wouldn't be able to sit at the lunch counter with me in this town, and he wouldn't be able to go to the bathroom marked "Men." I sat down next to Bill, trying to make sense of it all as I ate a sandwich with some potato chips and a cold drink.

After lunch, Dr. King came to the microphone. He spoke about nonviolent resistance and the work to be done in the future. Walking the protests, being beaten and pushed around, filling the jails; we will get there some day. People cheered as he spoke. "Six steps toward nonviolent social change," he said, and after handing the mike to one of the leaders, he said he had to go. The room suddenly fell quiet as he disappeared through the door.

With microphone in hand, the leader went to the black-board and summarized the six steps, which I copied down.

Step one. Information gathering. You first gather all the facts that you can about the conflict, to guide your campaign strategy.

Step two. Education. It is essential to share the information with the larger community, to minimize misunderstanding and gain support.

Step three. Personal commitment. Go over your commitment to the philosophy and methods of nonviolence. Eliminate hidden motives and prepare to accept suffering.

Step four. Negotiation. Confront the other party with a list of injustices and a plan for resolving them. Call forth the good in the opponent. Do not humiliate. Work toward a genuine meeting of minds.

Step five. Confrontation and direct action. This is used to force the opponent to continue dialogue to resolve injustice, and it is used to illustrate the injustice. There are many tactics for direct action, all used to impose a "creative tension" in the conflict, forcing the opponent to negotiate.

Step six. Reconciliation. Nonviolence does not seek to defeat or humiliate the opponent but seeks friendship and understanding. It is directed against evil systems and policies and not against people. Through compromise, one makes peace with the opponent and resolves the injustice with a plan of action.

After this talk we were divided into groups of six or eight people. I dreaded dividing up like this, but finally a group invited me in. We talked about nonviolence and loving one's enemy. In the middle of the discussion one man turned to me and said, "I can't be myself with you in here. I don't know whether you are from the KKK or some other infiltrator or what. I wish you would leave."

I was stunned. "I came here to learn about nonviolence," I said.

"Nonviolence? Shit. You people are responsible for all the violence."

I sat quietly for a moment, and then responded, "But I'm not."

"I'll show you your nonviolence," he said, getting up and ripping off his shirt to show scars on his back. "That's your nonviolence." I sat motionless, not saying a word.

"I'm not turning around until that man leaves," he announced to the group as he turned his chair around with his scarred back facing us. I was frozen with fear. The room became silent, everyone watching this tense drama.

All of a sudden I heard steps behind me and a cane reached all the way across the group and tapped the man on the shoulder. Like an explosion he jumped up, fists balled up, and lunged forward. There was Miriam facing him squarely, not backing up an inch. He glowered at her.

"Boy," she said, "you got a lot of learning to do about non-violence and white men. Now either you stay and start your learning or leave at once. Do you hear?" He towered over her but she stood there with her cane pointing up at him, as strong as a castle turret. All at once he slumped down, his body seeming to shrink.

"I'm getting the hell out of here," he said. As he left, Miriam turned around, and without looking at me, walked back to her group. Our group sat in silence for many moments.

"I'm sorry," I finally said. I'm not sure why I said that. I just needed to say something. "I'm sorry," I said again, perhaps this time realizing how much work there was yet for all of us to do. "I'm sorry," I finally said, breaking into the silence again, knowing how far I was from being able to love the enemy — an enemy who seemed to be sitting stiffly around me.

We sang more songs but at the end it all swirled around in my mind. I was greatly troubled and still frightened. I had neither felt nonviolent when the heat was turned on me nor had I been filled with love. I felt as if I had been put through an ordeal, an initiation rite, and had failed. I was still filled with fear and anger at the man in my group who had threatened me, and at those men who had led the bus exercise; I couldn't possibly fill my heart with love. How could I begin to move toward reconciliation and toward the beloved community? How did they do it? How could these people be so transformed that they could live with white people the life of the beloved community, after all that white people had done to them over the years and centuries?

I was afraid of committing myself to the way of nonviolence after this single day of feeling rejected and humiliated. I wanted to withdraw into familiar surroundings. I had learned a lot, but what I learned told me that I was not yet ready for a serious campaign of nonviolent resistance. It was much harder than I had imagined, and I was ashamed that I was so vulnerable to insult and incapable of the kind of love that would embrace and transform an embittered humanity. I was anxious to leave, and I looked around for Bill to drive me home.

As we left I searched for Miriam. I finally saw her standing beside the exit, leaning on her cane and eying everyone as they left. When I reached her I extended my hand. My eyes filled with tears.

"Welcome to the beloved community. You made it through with honor," she said, before I could say anything.

"I wouldn't say that, but thank you," I replied.

"Oh, it's my privilege to thank you. I've done some learning today. You have just begun. But you're still young yet. I hope you will find the freedom you are looking for before you're old like me. Learning comes hard. It comes with a lot of pain and suffering. But if you work at it, it finally comes. You helped me learn to love a white man. Now I am feeling more like a free woman today than I have in all these ninety-three years."

29

The Lively Office

DADDY AND MRS. KING left at four in the morning for a two-week vacation in July. I had gotten up early and prepared a small breakfast. Daddy King and I talked briefly about his vacation, mostly about what he was going to do. Then suddenly he was off.

I had no specific guidance about what my special responsibilities were to be while he was away and no specific instructions about caring for the house. I felt honored that they had the confidence in me to look after their house as well as to "pastor" their church in their absence. Dr. King was away at Martha's Vineyard, where he intended to be in seclusion writing a book.

When I arrived at Ebenezer that morning, the office was in a state of high commotion. Church people were milling around in the parking lot and on the front steps leading to the office. "What's going on?" I asked, as I pulled into my parking space.

"Rev is hurt," someone shouted.

"A huge car accident. Oh, Lord, help him."

"Lord, help us," people echoed.

I worked my way into the office through a crowd of people swarming around. I found Lillian with her head down on the desk rocking back and forth. "Lordy, Lordy, Lordy," she kept saying. Sarah was on the phone in the back of the office, being her efficient self. Suddenly the office grew silent as we became aware that Sarah was talking to the hospital. It was one of those phone calls in which everyone hung on each word, listening for hints of Daddy King's condition, but all Sarah said was, "Yes. Uh-huh. Okay. All right. Oh, my. Really? Yes." For a full five minutes, the crowd anxiously waited for news while Sarah clung to the phone without revealing anything. Finally she hung up the phone.

"Well," she said, "it looks like Rev has a broken leg and a broken arm." The group gasped and then waited for more news. "It seems that the limousine that picked him up at the airport had a serious accident with another car and Rev was hurt. At this point they don't know how bad, but they suspect just a broken leg and a broken arm. He is in stable condition. That was all they could tell me."

It was several hours before people finally began to leave the office. The phone rang incessantly as everyone in the church, it seemed, called in for the latest news. Soon the radio carried the reports and the public heard the news of the accident. The church became crowded again as many people stopped by the office seeking more information and the company of the parish family. By afternoon Lillian was on the phone with Reverend King in the hospital. He was in good spirits despite extreme pain.

It was several days before the office settled back to its normal routine. Reverend King was to be in the hospital for over a week and Dr. King would be coming back to Atlanta for the weekend to be in the pulpit for Sunday.

A few days later, I came to the church to take the boys from the youth group to the park to play softball. I wore old clothes and sneakers, which caused quite a stir in the youth group. "I came to play ball, not to preach," I told them.

"You play baseball?" they asked, as if they couldn't imagine that just a few years before I had played third base and left field for my high school team.

When we got to the field I took the bat and hit some grounders and flies to them. I said I would be the pitcher for both sides and they would pick the teams. I liked to pitch on occasions like this because I had a particular philosophy about pitching. I had found, in many sandlot games over the years, that the best athletes would pitch, and some of the younger youths and those without great athletic ability would strike out and walk away dejected. Instead of trying to get the batters out, I pitched so that everyone could hit, giving everyone a good chance at the plate. It would be up to the fielders to get them out.

I think they began to get the idea that this afternoon's play was not about winning but about making sure everyone had fun. It wasn't long before small bunches of boys gathered around the sidewalks with mitts and balls, all eager to play. At first we let some of them join our game to round out the teams, but soon we were just too many. We played a few happy innings until the score was about 31 to 27, reflecting lots of hits, lots of base running, and lots of errors.

The next day when I went to the office I saw Lillian looking at me oddly. Her head was tipped to one side as she watched me walk in. "What's going on?" I asked her.

"I just got a call from a white man last night. He talked to me awful nice, and at first I thought it was you."

"No, not me," I said.

"Well, I finally figured that out, because he wanted to jump into bed with me! He knew me, but I couldn't figure out who he was. Oh, I get calls from white men a lot," she said. "White men trying to take a little advantage of us."

"Isn't that the case," Sarah joined in.

Grimes, the custodian, had entered the office. He was always ready to tell a story and listen to a joke. "A while ago there was a woman named Myrabell," Lillian said. Grimes leaned on his mop and began to laugh as Lillian began. "Well,

Myrabell kept getting calls from this white man, and her husband didn't like it. But the white man didn't stop. One day she told the caller, 'Okay, I'll leave my bedroom lights on and you come on over.' She posted her husband outside in the shadows with his shotgun. He was so mad he would have blown that white man's brains out right then and there. But the man never came, and Myrabell's husband finally went to bed after waiting up half the night."

"Lordy, Lord," Sarah exclaimed. "Now that you mention her name, I think I remember them. Oh, yes, her husband would have done it too, and dropped the body off some bridge into a muddy river."

Grimes was already laughing, and it was clear a story was sprouting up inside him. He shifted his feet, leaned the mop against the other side of his face. "When I was in Japan in the war . . . " he said.

"Yes, yes," Sarah said, urging him on, knowing that somewhere soon in the story there would be a great laugh.

"Well," said Grimes, "I came upon a nice girl." He described how he'd gone out with her a few times just to get acquainted. "Pretty soon when my acquainting was over, you know . . . " he paused and began to laugh. "Yes, when my acquainting was over, I asked her."

"You did what?" asked Lillian.

"Well, I asked her real nice and she wouldn't do nothing." He laughed and laughed. "Can you beat that?" he exclaimed. "Nothing."

"Oh my," said Lillian, "you must have been mighty proud of her high moral nature."

Grimes paused and thought a moment. "Well," he finally said, "I would have been prouder . . . " he couldn't finish the sentence, he was laughing so hard. He bent over double and the mop fell to the floor with a crack. "Yes, I could have been prouder if her moral nature wasn't quite so high."

The door suddenly opened and into the office came Naomi King, Dr. King's sister-in-law, A. D.'s wife. She had one of her children in her arms and had stopped at the church on her way downtown, to go to the restroom. Grimes quickly picked up his mop and straightened himself up while Naomi began to laugh at the giggling faces in the office.

"Could you hold him a few moments?" she said to Lillian, handing her the baby. Lillian gladly took the baby and began rocking him gently, but he began to cry as soon as he saw his mother go out the door. Lillian stood up and began to sing.

> Into my heart, into my heart,
> Come into my heart, Lord Jesus.

The office suddenly was transformed into a sanctuary as she slowly walked around, rocking the baby and singing. Her voice was rich and full of feeling and it wasn't long before the baby stopped crying. I could see that Lillian had the touch.

"Well, I never thought I'd rock another generation of Kings," she said. "I used to smother Dr. King under these big boosies of mine and he would sleep there. I would rock him and sing to him for hours. I must have sung God's music right into his soul."

Soon Naomi returned to pick up her baby. She was a friendly person and always went out of her way to say a kind word to me. After she left, it took a little while for the office to get back to where it had been before she entered. Grimes came in and started to mop the floor again, but it was clear he was looking more for a good laugh than a piece of dirt. If he hung around long enough he usually found a little of both.

Several days later Daddy King returned to Atlanta. About twenty people from church met him and watched as he was eased into a special ambulance and brought home. I followed the ambulance to our home and helped him out and into his favorite chair.

It was then that the red pillow appeared. Daddy King propped his leg up on a bright red pillow, the brightest red that you could imagine. After that, everywhere he went in his wheelchair he used his big red pillow as a cushion for his leg.

"Look at this," he said while reading his mail one day. "Look at this, Bunch. Hey, Brewster, look at this," he called. Mrs. King and I rushed over to read the letter he was waving. It was a get well card from President Kennedy, with a little note and a signature.

"Now that will help a fella get well," he joked. "Now, he's a great man. I can feel my leg getting better already." He looked at his pillow as he held the card tightly in his hand. "I bet he would like my pillow, too."

30

Singing to Annette

TOWARD THE END of the summer I visited Annette again in the hospital. As a member of our youth group, we had been thinking about her and praying for her every week. I knew she was extremely ill, and I dreaded seeing her. Likely this would be the last time I would be with her, and I didn't know what to say. In spite of my fears I knew I had to go.

As I approached the nurse's station, one of the nurses smiled and said, "She's still here."

"Thank you," I replied.

Her door was open a crack, so I gently knocked, pushed it open, and walked in. She turned her head to see who it was and greeted me warmly with her large eyes. Her hand gestured welcome as I walked over to be beside her. Her arms were skin and bone, her eyes sunken, her flesh drawn tight across her face, but her lips and her eyes conveyed love as she recognized me and bid me welcome.

"Where is the dove?" I asked, looking at the window ledge. Smiling, she slowly shook her head, and I knew the pigeon hadn't returned. That pigeon had carried a lot of meaning to us both earlier in the summer. It had strutted boldly just outside her window, cooing as it went. Then it would suddenly fly off and as suddenly return with a big commotion of flapping and cooing. It had symbolized the dove from the Ark, flying out in search of the olive branch that would signify new life. I was sorry that it had not returned because it had given us the opportunity to talk on a symbolic level, in ways that others around us didn't understand.

"What beautiful flowers," I said, commenting on the many bouquets of flowers placed on every flat surface around the room, spilling over even onto the floor. They filled the room with their fragrance, welcome amid the strong smells of the hospital sickroom. I reached out and took Annette's hand. Her eyes looked huge and she just kept gazing at me with mysterious intensity.

A long moment of silence ensued. It was clear to both of us that she would not live long. I struggled to find the right words, because I had never been with a person so close to death, and I didn't know what to say. I was relieved when I saw her trying to say something, so I focused on her mouth, attempting to read the silent words off her dry lips. Suddenly I caught the phrase she was trying to say.

"Just as I am," I said, and she smiled. She raised her hand and gestured to her lips and it became clear that she wanted to sing the hymn. Then she pointed to me. "You want me to sing that hymn?" I laughed and she laughed too. "Okay," I said. "Let's sing together."

I then began to sing very quietly as she tightly squeezed my hand and shut her eyes.

> Just as I am, without one plea,
> But that Thy blood was shed for me,
> And that Thou bid'st me come to Thee,
> O Lamb of God, I come, I come.

That was the only verse I knew and she wanted me to sing it over and over. Tears welled up in my eyes, as I knew she was singing about herself: Just as I am, O Lamb of God, I come to you. Here I come, just as I am, and nothing more. Not the way I used to be, full of girlish laughter and play. Just as I am, I come, I come.

Annette smiled and I smiled through my tears. After singing this a number of times, she struggled to speak. This time
I heard the sound of her whisper, "Softly, softly."

"Ah," I replied, "Softly and Tenderly." She smiled and
squeezed my hand and at that I began to sing again.

> Softly and tenderly Jesus is calling,
> Calling for you and for me;
> See on the portals He's waiting and watching,
> Watching for you and for me.
>
> Come home, come home,
> Ye who are weary, come home.

When I got to this place the door suddenly opened and a
black nurse entered singing along with me.

> Earnestly, tenderly, Jesus is calling,
> Calling, O sinner, come home.

The nurse knew all the verses, and it seemed that at each
verse another one or two people joined us. Soon the room
was full, all of us holding hands and singing this hymn for
Annette.

> Why should we tarry when Jesus is pleading,
> Pleading for you and for me?
> Why should we linger and heed not His mercies,
> Mercies for you and for me?
>
> Come home, come home,
> You who are weary, come home;
> Earnestly, tenderly, Jesus is calling
> Calling, O sinner, come home.

By the time we had finished, all of us were crying. Because
we were holding hands and didn't want to break the circle, we

couldn't wipe our tears and hide them. Tears trickled down our faces and fell to the floor.

Annette closed her eyes and smiled faintly. It was a smile that seemed as if the angels had already surrounded her and were carrying her softly and tenderly home. One by one the nurses left and I remained for some time in silence, holding Annette's hand and watching and listening to her breathing.

A few weeks before, she had simply wanted to hear my voice as I talked to God, and I had learned from her to relax in my prayers and not to worry about specific words or my prayer formula. Now all she wanted was to hear me talk to God and sing the old hymns. First I was at a loss for words, but again she guided me into how I should be with her. I let the hymns become the prayers of this powerful ritual before death. She was sleeping now and her hand slowly lost its grasp.

"Good-bye, Annette. Softly and tenderly, Jesus is calling. Go home in peace."

I heard that Annette died a short time after we had sung to her. One of the nurses told me she died with the same smile on her face that she had when we were singing together and holding hands around her bed in the presence of the angels.

31

Unheeded Warning

TOWARD THE END of the summer, I was invited to speak at a small white church in the country about Dr. King and the civil rights movement. Always glad to speak about the issues of racism and my work at Ebenezer, I eagerly accepted. I swung into the parking lot for an evening meeting and looked around. I noticed that the church needed a coat of paint. I was looking forward to the evening as I opened the door and walked in.

The only person I saw was a black woman mopping the floor of the vestibule. As I approached her, a door swung open from a nearby office and a number of people emerged. As the woman pushed her mop in my direction I heard her whisper, with her head down and her eyes on the floor, "Be careful."

All at once about eight men surrounded me, warmly shaking my hand and welcoming me into their church. I was led into a meeting room and offered a cup of coffee. The room had a pungent smell of coffee and sweat and I gathered that these men had been meeting for a long time before I arrived.

The eight men ranged in age from about thirty to sixty and seemed eager to hear everything that I had to say. After introductions, I was invited to speak. "Tell us about the civil rights movement," they urged.

I smiled at everyone, trying to look at ease. But all I could hear were the ominous words "Be careful." What had the woman meant? Something inside me made me trust her words, but I didn't know how to follow them, surrounded by genial faces seemingly eager to listen. How could I speak about living with Reverend and Mrs. King and working with Dr. King and the people of Ebenezer and be careful?

I began by describing my seminary program as a white student working in the Ebenezer Baptist Church and how that fit into the larger civil rights movement. Then I described the lunch counter sit-ins that had started in Greensboro, North Carolina, in February. After that I talked about the Freedom Rides that only a few weeks before had run into violent mobs in Alabama. Then I talked about living with the Kings.

I had talked for about twenty minutes when a man interrupted me. "I just don't know what those people want, anyway."

That statement threw me off. I thought I had been making the point very clearly. While I was thinking how to answer this, the woman pushing the mop knocked on the open door.

"Be careful," she said, pausing on the word careful, "of the wet floor."

After she had gone, the man who had asked the question slowly got up and closed the door. I was quick to pick up what I thought was her signal to me, a second warning, but as brownies and a fresh round of coffee were passed around, her words didn't make things any clearer to me.

"Let's get back to my question," the man asked after he sat down. "What do these people want, anyway?" The way he said "anyway" disturbed me. There was more emotion in that word than would naturally flow from mere curiosity, yet to me the question was so simple that I was in my element answering it. I had been asked that question many times by white people this summer. What do black people want? How should I be careful?

"When you are thirsty and hot in downtown Atlanta," I asked, "what do you do?"

"I go into Rich's Department Store and have a soda at the lunch counter," he answered.

"When your children are of school age, how do you choose a school for them?"

"I look for the best school and enroll them," he said, and the others nodded in agreement.

"When you are traveling and you need to stop for the night, what do you do?"

"I go to a motel," he replied, seeming confused by my question.

"Okay," I said, "When your wives want to buy a dress in a department store and they aren't sure whether it will fit or not, what do they do?"

"They try on the dress, of course," several men answered.

A young, heavyset man leaned toward me. "I don't get your drift," he said.

"Yes, what are you driving at?" another chimed in.

I had learned how to be less fearful and more assertive over the summer, so I continued on.

"All these things that you do and take for granted no black person can do. The black women can't try on dresses in stores, members of my youth group can't buy drinks at Rich's lunch counter, their parents can't check into any motel along the highway. All they want is to be able to do what every white person can do in this country." I could feel my emotion beginning to well up as I confronted them with the evils I saw in the system. "They want to vote without being harassed."

"You'd better be careful, son, when you say that word around here. You are talking to some government officials in this room."

I suddenly knew that I had gone too far. I had stepped over the line. Who were these people? I had never asked and now it was too late, I thought. Why had they asked me out here?

"Recently, I talked to an elderly black Christian woman," I said, rolling on with hardly a pause, "and the most important goal in her time remaining, she said, is to learn how to love a white man after all they have done to her in her life."

"We get your drift," one person said.

"To love a white man," the heavyset man added in low tones. "I could take a little of that." An embarrassed silence fell over the room.

During the discussion that followed, I wondered how I could conclude and leave as quickly as possible, but they made it easy for me.

"Thank you for coming," one man said, breaking into a silence. The others stood up slowly and began to file out the door.

"Thank you for asking me," I replied. The meeting was over. I glanced into the dark sanctuary on my way out and the church seemed strangely threatening. "Thank you," I said again, as the church door closed behind me.

The parking lot was dark. As I walked over to my car, three men came out from behind a truck and stood in my way. I tried to walk around them, but they blocked my path. I recognized the heavyset man from the meeting. He must have slipped out a side door as I was getting ready to leave.

"You nigger-loving son of a bitch," he said. "He's one of those goddamn outside agitators from the North," he said to the others while looking right at me. I said nothing. He came so close to me, I thought he was going to hit me. I didn't move.

"What the hell shall we do with him?" a second man asked. The third man grabbed my shirtsleeve while I stood as quiet as I could. My heart pounded but I tried to conceal my terror by just standing limp and looking away. I wasn't going to run.

I wasn't going to fight. I was just going to stand there in the church parking lot and take their hostility. The image of the elderly woman from the nonviolent training conference flashed through my mind as she stood in front of the man whose fists were balled up ready to swing, so weak in her body yet so strong in the power of her love. "You've got it backward," she had told me. "Let your love cast out your fear."

All at once the church door opened. The three men vanished into the shadows behind trucks and cars as a shaft of light brightened up the parking lot. I looked around for someone from the church, but I only saw that shaft of light coming from the door. Then I heard the mop being struck against the door jam. Suddenly I got the picture. Oh, thank you, thank you, I said inaudibly to this mysterious angel who was looking out for me with a mop in her hand. Following the shaft of light, I got into my car and drove slowly down the driveway. When I reached the highway I put the accelerator to the floor. I was shaking all over.

The next morning I walked right into the SCLC office to see Dr. King. I had always made appointments before, but this time I was so desperate that I said I needed to see him right away.

At first the receptionist, whom I knew, told me I would have to wait, but then she caught the tone of my voice and went into Dr. King's office. "You may go in," she said, leading me through the doors and into his office.

Out of breath, I told him the story. "I felt like I was about to be beaten up by three white men in a church parking lot," I told him. "I stood limp as they debated what to do with me." He sat in silence in front of me.

"You have learned something about nonviolence," he finally said. "You didn't return violence for violence. 'Vengeance is mine,' says the Lord."

"That was the easy part," I replied, "How do you love those people, anyway?" I asked, echoing the word "anyway" that I heard spoken so vindictively the night before. "How do you love the enemy," I asked, "when all those people do such violent things to you? How do you still love them?"

He sat and thought. I was desperate for his answer. "How do you love the enemy?" I asked again, filling the silence with my question. "Turning your other cheek might be good tactics, but loving the person who hurt you is something else. How do you do it?"

I waited for his answer as phones rang and impatient knuckles rapped on the door. "Just a moment," he called to the person knocking on his door. Then he turned to me. "You've got to reach deeper," he said softly, "until you are transformed by your suffering. With your suffering and your love, you must cut the chains of hate. You've got to reach down deeper until your suffering and love draw you closer to God."

The door opened. "It's the Justice Department," his secretary said.

"Thank you for coming in, ya hear?"

"Thank you," I replied. I shook his hand, and giving way to the Department of Justice, I left.

Reach deeper, I kept saying as I drove off, until I am transformed by my suffering. Reach deeper until my suffering and love draw me closer to God. This is how I am to learn to love those people in the parking lot.

My seminary education never brought me this far. I hardly knew where to begin. I had learned something about the tactics of nonviolence, but the parts about transforming suffering and about love that cuts the chains of hate was not yet embedded in my bones. Hatred seemed inevitably to spring from fear, vengeance was always a tempting response to hurt, and violence and more violence in my culture of violence was the easiest action of all against violence. Men understood that. They waited for it.

But how can violence itself be stopped? This is the central question. Violence destroys everyone it touches, Dr. King had said in a sermon. Only love can overcome violence; loving one's enemies, loving enough that true reconciliation can take place, suffering and loving so much that we suffer and love the beloved community into existence. Loving this way is humanity living the divine way of life on earth. I wasn't yet there, but what else could I do but reach deeper and try? I had to admit that perhaps some of my best teachers had been those three angry men threatening me as I stood limp on the cement of that church parking lot, demanding that I reach deeper, beyond any depth I had ever known before, into the well of suffering and love.

32

The Hope of the World

"**B**REWSTER, don't forget my pillow," Daddy King called out to me as he rolled out on his wheelchair toward his car. I went inside and brought his red pillow to him. Clearly in great pain, he eased his broken leg into a comfortable position.

"Now, now, now," he said, grimacing. "Now, now, now." We knew that he said this only when the pain became intense. "We're going to hear M. L. this morning. I wonder what he will tell us today."

When we arrived at the church the buzz and hum of activity was everywhere. Children were being escorted to church school and the choir was practicing in the basement. Everyone was beautifully dressed, the men in dark suits and ties and the women looking sharp in their colorful hats.

A small group of men tried to wheel Daddy King into the church. With his leg propped up high on his bright red pillow he caused a great stir, and people swarmed around him. Mrs. King kept urging him on as she greeted everyone. "I'll get there, Bunch," he kept saying.

I went up to Dr. King's office to find him and help prepare for the service. He was seated behind the desk, going over his notes. He showed me the text he was preaching from, and the morning's bulletin. I was to do the pastoral prayer and read the story of Sodom and Gomorrah from Genesis.

"The hope of the world is in a creative minority," he said, pointing to his notes. "The hope of the world," he mused.

With our robes on, we checked our watches and began to walk toward the sanctuary. We could hear the choir and the organ and the singing of the congregation. Upon hearing all these happy sounds I suddenly became nervous about saying the pastoral prayer.

It had been only six weeks before that I was suddenly called on to pray before this congregation and had been guided through the words by the ACTS formula. Annette, lying in her hospital bed, had challenged my stilted form of extemporaneous prayer as I prayed beside her one afternoon, using the formula. "I just want to hear you talk with God," she had whispered to me in her frail and failing voice. "Yes, you just talking with God."

I knew now that people simply wanted to hear me talk to God. And they wanted to be brought into this conversation with their hearts and minds. I knew I had to reach beyond the beautifully written prayers in the Book of Common Prayer to a place in my heart that was authentic and alive. Just in case my nervousness reduced me to the briefest pastoral prayer in history, to a series of empty, lifeless words, I had scratched a few points to remember, on a three-by-five card.

Dr. King opened the door and all at once we emerged from a small hidden corridor onto the platform. Dr. King and I took our seats beside each other, just in front of Lillian and Sarah who sat with the choir. Looking out over the congregation, I saw members of my youth group scattered here and there in the pews. Several waved to me in a friendly greeting. Mother Clayton sat near the front on my right side, her eyes taking everything in, her face registering no visible emotion. Like a queen bee, she was surrounded by three or four women attendants who showed her great respect and affection. She held her purse tightly on her lap, ready to signal her feelings about the church to the women around her.

Daddy King was in his wheelchair, his leg propped high on his red pillow for all to see. He was singing heartily when we entered and as he turned to see us enter, he twisted his leg. "Now, now, now," he exclaimed. It was clear by how he sang and moved his arms and body that he was still leading the service, no matter where he sat or who was on the platform.

Soon Dr. King and I were singing and soon I was giving the pastoral prayer. This time the words flowed easily, and as people prayed out loud in response to my words, I just kept praying. I talked with God as Annette had led me to do and brought the congregation into this dialogue with me and into this conversation with God. I could feel the people I loved praying right along with me, encouraging me to reach deeper and deeper into my faith and far beyond my notes. After I concluded my prayer, I began to read the lesson for the day, about Abraham bargaining with God. When I finished, Dr. King came to the pulpit to preach.

"The hope of the world is in a creative minority," he said, speaking slowly and deliberately, emphasizing each word. No sooner had he finished this sentence than a chorus of voices shouted out from around the church.

"Preach, brother," "Yes, Lord," "Tell it like it is, brother," "Save us, Jesus," and countless other expressions issued forth from the hearts of people, filled with expectation and eager for a word of hope.

"How many good men are needed to save the city?" he asked.

"How many?" a man right behind me shouted from the choir. "Tell us."

"How many good men are needed to save the city?" Dr. King asked again, and again he paused, letting the shouts of encouragement fill the air.

It became clear to me that we were not just listening to Abraham struggle over the fate of Sodom; we were listening to Dr. King struggle with our nation's leadership over the fate of this country. How many good people does it take to turn this country around? How many does it take to turn God's face from judgment into compassion? How many, at a time when God's judgment seemed to fall so heavily upon the nation and world? These were good questions. The sanctuary was alive.

Dr. King painted in words and images a dynamic portrait of Abraham standing before God, bartering. " 'Would fifty do?' Abraham asked. 'Fifty righteous people. Fifty good people?'

" 'Yes,' said God. 'I will not destroy the city for the sake of fifty righteous people.'

" 'How about forty-five? Forty-five good people. Would you save Sodom if you found forty-five good people in the city? Will you destroy the city and not save the righteous?' "

A chorus of voices rose up from the congregation. "Tell us," "Yes, Lord," "Preach the truth, brother."

" 'Now, God,' " Dr. King said, acting out Abraham's argument, " 'you are a just God. Will you destroy those righteous people along with the wicked? Will you treat the righteous in just the same way that you treat the wicked? Do you call this justice?' "

A chorus of no's shot forth from the sanctuary.

" 'No,' said God, 'for the sake of the righteous I will not destroy the city.'

" 'Oh, forgive me,' " Dr. King said, following Abraham's argument. " 'Let me ask you again. Suppose thirty righteous people are found in the city. Will you destroy it if you found thirty?' "

"No," a chorus of voices began to shout. "Save it, Jesus."

" 'No,' God said. 'If I find thirty good people I will not destroy the city.' "

"Thank you, Jesus."

"Praise the Lord."

Dr. King paused as he sensed the rising emotion. " 'Do not be angry with me, O just God,' " Dr. King went on. " 'Do not be angry with me if I ask you again. Will you destroy the city if you found twenty righteous people, just twenty good people?'

" 'No,' said God. 'I will not destroy it if I find twenty.' " By this time the congregation was filled with excitement as people were calling out to God, Dr. King, their neighbors, and everyone within earshot to urge Abraham on so the city would be saved.

" 'O God,' " Dr. King called out, " 'withhold your anger if I speak to you just once again. Do not be angry with your faithful servant if I speak to you just once more. Suppose, O God, there are ten good people in the city. Will you destroy it then?'

" 'No,' God answered, 'I will not destroy it for the sake of ten.' " At this the congregation cheered and cheered.

"After that, God went away and Abraham went home."

Dr. King paused to shift his emphasis. "There were probably more than fifty good people in Sodom," he said, "but theirs was an irrelevant goodness. There were more than fifty good people but they were conventionally good, obsessed with the rules of respectability. More than fifty, but these were negatively good. More than fifty, but these were watchfully good. More than fifty, but these were narrowly good."

He expanded on each kind of goodness as the congregation shouted and urged him on. Each time he repeated the rhythm of a preceding phrase, his voice grew louder and more intense. Finally he paused again while the people kept shouting.

"Ten men could save Sodom," he finally said, "just ten men. This echoes a timeless and timely truth that the saving force in any group, committee, or civilization is a creative minority."

By this time his preaching had developed such force that people everywhere began to stand up and shout. Many waved their arms. Several fell backward and were helped back down into their seats or gently laid on the floor in the aisles.

"God found one man — just one man, whose name was Lot." At this the people shouted as Dr. King rose to his highest level of intensity. Suddenly a woman cried out, and seizing her hair in her hand, pulled off her wig, and threw it in the air. This was followed by another and then another. Soon cries came from everywhere and wigs flew high in the air all over the sanctuary.

I recalled Lillian telling me that she always knew Dr. King was really preaching when the wigs came off. "You'll know he's preaching, Brewster, when the wigs begin to fly."

Bringing the congregation back down, Dr. King began to lower his voice, repeating his point and driving it home. "The hope of the world lies in that minority that will do what is right rather than what is expected. So God remembered Abraham and brought Lot out of the city before he destroyed Sodom. He couldn't find ten good men in that whole city."

He paused as if he were looking for ten good people in the United States government, ten people who would be a creative minority that would save this country, and he hadn't found ten in high places who visibly supported the cause for justice.

"And God brought fire down upon the city because God couldn't even find ten good people. But God found Lot and Lot became the saving force, that minority who will do what is right rather than what is expedient. The hope of the world lies in a creative minority."

At this point, after about an hour of preaching, there were quiet murmurs of "Amen," "Yes, Lord," "Thank you, Jesus," "Praise God." Then the organ began to play quietly.

I sat spellbound, not five feet from him. The beauty and power of his rhetoric deeply moved me. He made a person

want to go out and march; one felt the drumbeats in his cadences. His ideas sparkled with imagery. I was in awe of his
ability to quote from great people in literature: Shakespeare,
Dryden, Lincoln, Homer, and Nietzsche, to name a few mentioned in this sermon. He combined emotional power with
wisdom, drawing from a wide range of sources that he had
gleaned from his liberal arts education. His delivery was a
symphony, rising to a crescendo and then slowly subsiding,
bringing the congregation back down again. When I looked
out at the congregation I saw tears rolling down people's
cheeks as fast as they were wiped away and people openly
comforted each other.

New members were welcomed, prayers were offered up,
and more hymns were sung. When the collection was taken,
I watched Mother Clayton closely as she opened her purse,
and I saw the curious glances of the women watching her,
some trying to be discreet as they peeped out of the corner
of their eye, while others leaned almost pushing one another
to get a better look. Soon the service was over. I noticed that
Dr. King had left his sermon notes on the podium, so I picked
them up in my hand as I left. When we got up in his office,
he talked to me about his sermon.

"All the people won't go with you, Brewster," he said.
"Sometimes you have to act alone, wherever you are. God
is looking for a creative minority to change our churches and
to govern this country. God is looking for a creative minority
to change the world."

As we left to greet people, I wondered whether I could be
part of that creative minority. Walking down the hall with
him I prayed over and over, "Help me, God, to be part of
your creative minority."

33

Farewell

THE FLURRY of activity during my last week in Atlanta began with a memorable breakfast. Right on schedule I went through my established routine, first letting Tappy out to chase squirrels in the yard and then getting a few strips of bacon sizzling in the pan and grits cooking on the back burner.

"I'm sure looking forward to meeting your Martha," Daddy King said as he descended the stairs. He had observed me sending and receiving many letters over the summer, which had drawn much attention, and her photograph, which I kept on my desk at church, had drawn many admiring comments. "You bring her right over here," he said.

In fact, everyone wanted to meet Martha, and I had received a lot of teasing in the office. She was to arrive in a few hours, so I had to plan her entrance carefully.

"Have you ever thought of becoming a Baptist?" Daddy King asked as we sat down to eat. "You fit in so well right here that I think you'd make a mighty fine Baptist."

"I like the Baptist tradition a lot," I answered, "but at the moment I plan to stay an Episcopalian. Episcopalian with a Baptist flair," I joked.

Mrs. King drew up to the table. "Brewster," she said, having heard our conversation, "King's right. You'd make a good Baptist." She sipped her coffee and looked at me. "Would you consider coming back here after you graduate and working with us at Ebenezer? Daddy King and I have been talking about it. People like you and they would like you to return."

I sat in silence for a moment, amazed. Overwhelmed, I finally responded, "Thank you. What a happy thought. I will have to see, when I graduate."

"Of course," Daddy King said. "You take your time deciding."

"I would love to come back. I'll let you know," I added. My mind began to spin at the thought. The church sign and the letterhead would read "King, King, and Brewster." I was in awe at their invitation and at the possibility of working with them both in their church. The fact that Mrs. King initiated the invitation, indicating that they had talked together, moved me deeply. I didn't know what to do except to say thank you. I broke the silence by going to the stove to fill my plate with grits and bacon.

When I came back to the table I revealed a little plan I had been hatching. "You have often said that this house needs more trees in front. I have gone to a nursery and have bought you a present of a good-sized oak tree. Pick the right place for it and I'll see that it is delivered and properly planted. This is in appreciation for all the wonderful things you have done for me this summer. A tall, solid oak tree." They were amazed by this gesture and said I shouldn't have done such a thing. "I've already bought it," I said. "Picked out just the one I wanted. When I come back, I will want to see the oak tree standing tall, able to provide you with a little shade. The earliest the nursery can deliver it is next week, after I've gone, so we've got to find a good place for it."

Soon we were outside walking around the front yard, trying to figure out the best place to put the oak tree. "How about here?" Mrs. King said. I picked up a small rock and placed it on the spot. We stood back and looked.

"Fine," Daddy King said. "Looks good to me. A mighty oak tree. That will look just fine." I was pleased that they took to my idea so enthusiastically, and I was sorry it could not be delivered and planted that very day.

Later that day I picked up Martha at the airport and drove her through downtown Atlanta and up Auburn Avenue to Ebenezer Baptist Church. I showed her Rich's Department Store, where I had had my first experience with segregated lunch counters and bathrooms, and drove her past the swimming pool where I had been prevented from taking the youth group to swim.

When we arrived at the church, Lillian and Sarah burst out of the door to greet us. Grimes, too, came running up with mop in hand. Inside there was a great commotion. Lillian looked Martha over and walked around her, like somebody about to buy a horse, laughing all the way.

"She looks good, Brewster," she exclaimed. "How did you find such a fine young lady?"

"My, oh my," Sarah blurted out slapping the table. "She's mighty pretty."

Grimes didn't say much but he looked and nodded his head and grinned in approval. After the initial greetings I showed Martha my office and her photograph on the desk. Lillian and Sarah made lots of comments about silly things about me I hadn't realized they had noticed.

"Better call on Rev. He's upstairs," Lillian advised.

As we ascended the stairs to the office, I realized I hadn't told Martha about how Daddy King conducted premarital sessions. He had told me on several occasions how, after he sized up a couple, he would tell them whether to get married or not. With fire in his eyes, he told me, he would tell couples not to marry if he didn't think they belonged together. He would be so forceful that they had to listen. He would hold nothing back. Subtlety was not part of his game plan.

As I led Martha into his office I knew that sooner or later I would hear what he thought of the two of us. Even though Martha and I hadn't mentioned the idea of marriage in our conversations with each other, people at Ebenezer were quick to jump to this conclusion. "Is this the one?" they kept asking me, and then they burst into laughter. "Is this the real one?" I knew I was in for some awkward moments because I hadn't brought the subject up to her yet. "Hard to say," I would reply with a laugh. "Mighty hard to say."

The meeting with Daddy King went well. Perhaps he sensed my nervousness because he was gentle with his questions. He asked her about her summer in which she had taught swimming to children and adults at a quarry near her house. He was interested in her seminary studies and her program at Union Theological Seminary. She had planned to study world religions but had to leave in her first year to care for her father after her mother died. She had a deep faith, Daddy King found out, and was a committed Christian.

He would rock back in his tilting chair and think, and then ask another question. "Do you love this man?" he asked. "Oh, no," I said to myself, hoping he would not pursue this question too far. She looked at me and blushed. "Yes," she said. He paused, and then it seemed that his mind went off in another direction, letting this topic rest.

It soon became clear to me that he and Martha liked each other a lot. The room was full of laughter and warm welcomes. When we walked down the hall to the main office, we heard the typewriters stop long before we reached the door. Lillian and Sarah were both looking at us with big grins on their faces. They were eager to hear all the details. "Well, Brewster?" they asked. They gathered around as if they were awaiting a big announcement. I merely said, "Everything went just fine. Just fine."

I liked keeping them in a little suspense, because I knew what they were thinking. If they felt any disappointment, they didn't reveal it. I knew they had been waiting for a marriage announcement, but this was not to be, for another three months. Now I knew they couldn't wait until Martha and I had left so they could have a major caucus about their impressions of us.

After showing Martha around the sanctuary, I took her up to the platform where I sat on Sundays. "This is where I will preach," I told her, mentioning the sermon I was to deliver in two days. "I'm scared out of my wits."

We drove to the house of one of the parishioners, where Martha would spend the next two nights. After settling her in, we got into the car for a tour of Atlanta. Soon we were driving out to Bill and Esther Turner's house in the country. I had seen a good deal of them over the summer, and Esther had been a very important support for me. Over the course of the summer she and I had talked about many things. She was the only white member of Ebenezer and had been deeply involved with the church and the civil rights movement in Atlanta for a number of years. It was important for me that Martha meet both Esther and Bill.

I warned Martha that the only physical ailment that I had had all summer was the chiggers that had discovered me in Esther's pastures. I had never encountered chiggers before, and as I walked I was completely unaware of how they would burrow under my tender skin. The next day, when I began to itch desperately, Mrs. King came to my rescue. She gave me her nail polish and told me to dab a little over each sore to smother them out. She had always looked after me in a most kind way.

When I got home that night I worked on my sermon again, but I grew more and more nervous about it. I still was not one who could speak without extensive notes, so I wrote it all out, word for word. I envied those preachers who, like Dr. King, could talk for an hour or more without notes. I was afraid that I might not articulate my thoughts in just the right way, or that I might even forget important points. I went over my manuscript many times, trying to free myself from the text, but still I knew I had to have it all typewritten in front of me. Besides, the Ebenezer congregation was used to sermons lasting about an hour; I couldn't imagine holding their attention for even thirty minutes. Reverend King and Dr. King would just be warming up after thirty minutes of preaching; I was afraid I would end before people really began to listen.

And then it was Sunday morning and I was on the platform, beside Daddy King in his wheelchair with his leg propped up on the bright red pillow. I read the Gospel, said the pastoral prayer, and all at once the pulpit was mine. I looked out over the congregation and saw my friends sprinkled here and there throughout the sea of people. I saw Martha looking at me, full of support. Suddenly someone shouted, "Let's hear it, preacher." I felt like jumping though the roof.

I hadn't even settled myself with a moment of silence before a chorus of calls rang through the sanctuary. "Amen, Jesus," "Tell it like it is."

"Make it plain, Brewster," Daddy King called out. "Make it plain, Brewster." I learned to cherish these words.

I could hear Sarah from the choir right behind me saying, "Yes, Lord," and I hadn't even started the sermon yet. I began to feel as if people were cheering me on all through the congregation, supporting me, uplifting me, urging me to be as bold and dynamic as I could be. They were calling the Divine Spirit to rain down and inspire me and to reconnect the congregation to God's vision. I felt the weight of this responsibility, and my own inadequacy. Amid the chorus of support I prayed silently for guidance and the strength to carry it out, and then I began.

Over the course of the summer I had come to expect approving calls from the congregation, but during this service it seemed different. The chorus was intense, the shouting was loud. I leaned into them and they held me aloft. A great conversation was taking place among the Holy Spirit, the congregation, and me. No one fell over, however. No wigs flew in the air, no wild screams arose from depths of grief or ecstasy, and there were no dramatic responses to my words like those that Dr. King and Daddy King evoked. To the congregation my preaching must have seemed tame and subdued. To me, on the other hand, their involvement was exhilarating. As I preached, I felt more and more alive, getting away from my text to repeat phrases for emphasis, to tell a story that I hadn't planned, or to find a rhythm in my words that brought forth their responses.

The experience of preaching from the pulpit where three generations of the King family had preached moved me deeply. The sanctuary seemed filled with the spirits of Reverend Williams, Daddy King, and Dr. King and filled with the spirits of those throngs who for nearly half a century had gathered there to praise the Lord.

I preached about gratitude, my gratitude for their support all summer long; about love, and how important it was to love during this period of racial unrest; and about hope and confidence that God will sustain us on our journeys. As I neared the close, the organ started to play softly, lifting my words into music and carrying them aloft. A hymn grew out of the organ's improvisation and people joined in, humming at first, and then singing the verses and chorus aloud. As I listened to the singing I felt tears welling up in my eyes and I just let them be.

After the service, a farewell reception was prepared. Many people spoke, including Daddy King and several members of the EYO. They showered presents on me — a set of handkerchiefs, neckties, and a briefcase, among other things. The farewells lasted a long time; it was hard to say good-bye. A line formed as I gave and received many hugs. All at once it was over.

I had cleared my office on Friday of all my summer's accumulations and had said good-bye to Lillian and Sarah and to Grimes and his family. I had also said good-bye to my friends Esther and Bill. I was leaving an empty church, and I felt strange. Just moments before it was reverberating with energy, and now it was quiet. Just moments before I had been speaking in ways that only eight weeks before I could not have imagined. How different I felt. I realized that I was saying farewell to that place and to those people who had changed me profoundly. I knew that I was leaving a sacred place that had blessed me in ways that I could not yet begin to comprehend.

I said farewell and I took Martha to the Kings for my final visit with them. I wish I had cranked a freezer full of peach cream for Reverend King as my parting gift, but, alas, there just wasn't time. Our dinner was soon over and we said good-bye. As I turned to get into my car, I gave Tappy, my faithful early-morning companion, a little pat. Then I gave a farewell wave and Martha and I headed north, toward the Drinking Gourd into the future.

34

Epilogue

MORE THAN FORTY-FIVE YEARS separate me from that moment when I raised my hand in the seminary classroom, waved it vigorously, and heard those fateful words, "Brewster gets Ebenezer."

What does this part of my life mean, now that I look back on the experience? There is a river running deep underground, which carries the spirit of the Ebenezer of 1961 in my soul.

I returned from the summer to my mother, who welcomed the change she saw in me even though I hadn't realized what a spiritual transformation I was living through. I quickly saw for myself how much I had changed when I preached in the seminary chapel. No shouts of encouragement filled my ears, no "amens," no "thank you, Jesus," or "preach to me," or, "make it plain, Brewster," which Daddy King used to chant back to me as I preached. As we sang the hymns, ringing in my ears were those haunting questions asked of me just a few weeks before, "Well, Rev, what do you have to sing about? The white folks left some of us behind when they crossed the river. How do you sing about that? Do you ever sing the sorrow songs of your people? Do you ever sing of your struggles?"

I had become changed to the point where fitting in was very painful but I was too shy, perhaps, and felt too alone in my ideas and feelings to become outwardly expressive. I now saw the world with new eyes, through the eyes of Mother Clayton, Grimes, Lillian and Sarah, and of course, Daddy King and Dr. King, as well as countless other people who cried out for freedom now and not later, freedom here and not in some distant place, whose needs were real and whose transcendent vision of hope drove them forward. I wondered how I would fit into the church without becoming so tamed that this new vision of hope would become unrecognizable.

After seminary, Martha and I were married. Shortly afterward, we both went to India, where we worked for two years at the Madras Christian College. Upon our return in 1964, I became the assistant to the Episcopal chaplain at Cornell University. Four years later I became the Episcopal chaplain and remained at Cornell until 1999.

It was not long before I heard Dr. King's voice again, this time calling people from across the country to join him in what was to become the great march over the Edmund Pettus Bridge from Selma to Montgomery. Responding to his call, I soon found myself marching with more than twenty-five thousand people, with the numbers swelling the closer we came to Montgomery. "We're on the move now to the land of freedom," he shouted from the steps of the capitol. The atmosphere was wild with energy, "How long?" he asked. "Not long," we shouted back. "How long?" he shouted even louder and we shouted back even louder still, "Not long." Soon black and white, old and young, rich and poor were locking arms and singing "We Shall Overcome," inspired once again that masses of people gathering for a great cause could change the course of history.

Only a few months after that I was surprised to open a letter from Mrs. King Sr. asking if I would consider becoming the associate minister at Ebenezer, with Daddy King and Dr. King. I was shocked. They had hinted at this in 1961 but now it was a real job offer. Soon word came from both Daddy and Dr. King saying that they wanted me to join them on their staff.

The civil rights movement had moved far in the five years between 1961 and 1966. I had been welcomed in 1961 in a breakthrough position as a white minister working in a black southern church, but now the mood was different. Malcolm X had become a voice for vigorous change before his assassination, and Stokely Carmichael just a few months before had championed the phrase "Black Power." Was nonviolence no longer the best way to force change on the entrenched white system? I feared that my presence would be the cause of resentment rather than a springboard toward reconciliation.

After serious deliberation, my wife and I decided not to accept the permanent position but instead to spend the summer in Atlanta. This time Lillian Watkins, Ebenezer's senior administrator for many years, invited us to stay with her. "But Lillian," I said, "we have a two-month-old baby, a two-year-old daughter, and our huge Newfoundland dog."

"O honey," she replied, "I can give you a back yard for your dog, and one room for your family. If your family can take me, I can live with you." What a summer we had living with her in that one room with our children, and in the immense heat without an air conditioner. Lillian always walked around with a quart canning jar of ice-cold water, which she kept filling and loading again with ice.

Indeed, the mood was different that summer as fires broke out frequently in black neighborhoods and bomb threats came to individuals and institutions with alarming regularity. An integrated preschool and kindergarten classroom that Martha had worked in was burned to the ground the night before it was to open. She had juggled her time between that program and directing a drama, *Circle beyond Fear,* by Darius L. Swann, for the Ebenezer Youth Organization, but now she was fearful to drive alone at night. People were afraid and cautious, and the presence of a white person in the black community caused suspicion.

One day, a man with whom I had frequently spoken in 1961, who lived on a side street near the church, was sitting on his front steps. I went up to him and we began to talk. At one point in our conversation he pulled his pants tight against his leg, and I could see the outline of a gun held in a holster against his skin. "I'm Black Power now," he said. "Nobody messes with me." I felt a sudden shot of adrenalin charging through my body, as fear seized me for an instant. "But how do you create peace with a gun," I asked. He shrugged. I pressed on. "How do you break the cycle of violence with a gun?" "Maybe that's for them," he said emphatically, "but it ain't for me."

"How do you keep going out there?" I wanted to ask Dr. King, "when police dogs bite you, when the jet blasts from high-power hoses throw you to the ground, and when white police painfully twist your arm behind your back? How do you keep going out there when your children are cursed and discriminated against? How do you love your enemies when they inflict so much violence against you? What keeps you going, Dr. King?"

When those questions surfaced, Dr. King was far away. He was in Chicago, then in San Francisco, Los Angeles, and New York; then home in Atlanta, but soon away again. I longed for a quiet time when I could probe these deep questions with him the way I had done before, but that time would never come.

I knew that my relationship to the man in the street changed into a relationship of fear after I saw the outline of his gun against his leg, shouting out loud with no ambiguity, "Nobody messes with me." I wondered what I could do. With the power of his gun silently confronting me, I could feel my heart slowly back away. He had a gun and I simply had a vulnerable body and the powerful idea of nonviolence that had suddenly become fragile. It was an idea that many people now felt had become outmoded. We could no longer talk easily together, and as I walked away, a wave of sadness came over me.

How can violence itself be stopped? This great question kept alive by Dr. King, has all but vanished in our time, like steam from a boiling pot. Whether it is a gun strapped to a man's leg or an atomic bomb trigger ready in a launching pad, the command — don't mess with me — tends to drive out the principle of loving one's enemies as the way of creating justice and peace. Some say that the only way to bring parties to the bargaining table is though threats of violence and more threats of violence. Could we talk as equals only if I carried a gun? That conversation, however, would leave my heart behind. My enemy would likely never become my friend, and we would never become partners in creating a new world together, as Dr. King would say. The reliance on armed confrontation as the only option in settling great human struggles keeps us from trying to answer this question. Certainly peace as an end can't be stopped by using violence as a means to that end. The question — how can violence itself be stopped? — hangs over the conversations of the human race like an unheeded cloud before thunder.

"It is much easier to go into a back room and buy a gun for a few dollars than it is to put your life on the line in the name of nonviolence," this man in the street said to me. How quickly, I thought, the vision involving love and suffering, as well as discipline and incredible perseverance, vanishes in our country where violence comes so naturally as a way of settling differences and exerting power and control.

After spending the summer of 1966 in Atlanta, I heard from Ebenezer again on that devastating day of April 4, 1968, the day Dr. King was killed. I quickly flew to Atlanta. "I was expecting you," Daddy King said to me as we solemnly met at his house. "It's bad, Brewster, bad. I don't understand it. Why did they kill him? I am hurt by this, hurt in many ways;

hurt too bad I don't know how I'll ever get over it. I don't think I can." Mrs. King came up to us. "I don't know what happened," she said. "It isn't real. I read the papers and they say two hundred thousand people will come for my baby. I don't know what has happened."

I returned to Daddy King's house the day before Dr. King's funeral, because he had asked me to drive him to the funeral service of an elderly parishioner, which was taking place the day before Dr. King's funeral. Daddy King wanted me to stop at his son's gravesite on the way, and in silence we drove to the South View Cemetery, where Dr. King was to be buried. We walked around the gaping hole in the ground with tears rolling down our cheeks. A few mourners were there as well as some men with overalls and shovels. They stepped back as we walked around the gravesite. Daddy King nodded to the people and thanked the men who had dug the grave. We both got into the car and as we sat down, I reached over and touched his arm. "My boy, my boy," he said, with tears flowing down his cheeks. He then clenched his fists as if forcing his tears to stop and I didn't see his tears again until Dr. King's funeral was over.

"You'd better save a seat for yourself," Daddy King said to me on the day of Dr. King's funeral. After parking my car, I entered the sanctuary and located a seat. "Saved for Reverend Brewster," I wrote in large letters, and then climbed the back stairs to Lillian and Sarah's office. The choir was rehearsing, some people were busy with preparations, and many others were just milling around in silence, just wanting to be near other people, to be part of the grieving heart of Ebenezer.

After the funeral, a mass of people began to walk down Auburn Avenue in the memorial march. Feeling immense pain and grief I wanted to be alone, so I worked my way against the flow of people toward my car, and silently I drove away, watching the massive crowd make its way down the street toward a very different world. It would be a world in which the puzzle pieces of my life and the puzzle pieces of America did not easily fit together anymore. This was to be a world without Dr. King, a world where people dared not ask questions about violence and nonviolence and dared not talk about suffering for a transcendent cause. Where had the spiritual foundation gone that was necessary to sustain such a powerful movement of faith and action?

In 1979, I invited Daddy King to visit Cornell for a weekend as a guest of the university and the Episcopal Church at Cornell. By that time, his other son, A. D., had died in a swimming pool accident in 1969, and Mrs. King, his wife, had been killed in 1974. She had been playing the organ before the service when a gunman opened fire on the congregation. He was quickly subdued but too late to save her life. Reverend King hadn't traveled much after that.

"Preach here the way you preach at Ebenezer," I whispered to him as I escorted him to the pulpit. When he got to the pulpit, he rested his elbow on it and leaned far out staring intently at the congregation of the Episcopal Church at Cornell. I knew we were in for something unusual. I could barely imagine the pain he had endured through all those family tragedies during the intervening years, and I wondered how those tragedies had affected his faith and his spirit.

He started quietly, but then I could feel his energy beginning to rise. He voice grew louder and louder as he looked out at us with the eyes of an eagle. Then down onto the pulpit came his hand with a loud crash as he made his point. The children, whom I had placed in the front rows, nearly jumped out of their seats. His voice rose, and again and again his hand crashed down on the pulpit. Suddenly the children burst out laughing. He paused, looking first at them and then at me and back to them as they giggled uncontrollably. "What's the matter?" he asked, looking directly at me. "Don't you preach, Brewster?"

In 1979 I invited Daddy King to preach at Cornell University. Before he began, I whispered in his ear, "Preach here like you preach at Ebenezer." (Photos by Hadley Smith, used with permission.)

Hadley Smith

The foundations of Anabel Taylor Hall shook that day as they had never shaken before. Toward the end of his sermon, his voice grew quiet and he paused. A very different mood came over him, and we waited for what he would say next. Moments ticked away. "I lost my first son, M. L.," he said, pausing again. "Then I lost my second son a year later." He followed this with a longer pause, all the while looking out at the congregation as if searching the souls of everyone present. "Then," he said finally, "I lost my wife. I have lost so much, but I can always imagine that I could lose more. I could have turned into a man of hate. I could have turned into a man against God. I could have turned away from life because God has taken so much from me." He paused, and we waited anxiously for his next words. "But God has given me even more, so I am grateful." He paused again, looking out at us. "God has taken much away from me, but God has given to me even more. I am a grateful man. No one can take my gratitude away from me."

He was quiet again. This was even a longer pause, long enough for the congregation to become nervous. Everyone waited for what he would say next. Finally looking out over the congregation, he simply said, "Brewster is like a son to me."

I was absolutely shocked. I sat there stunned, tears filling my eyes. I had had no idea he felt this way. All along in the early days, when I made breakfasts for him, I knew he meant a lot to me and I knew we got along well, but it was hard for me to imagine what I might have meant to him, or what it meant for him to take a white man into his home for a summer. I had not really looked at the relationship from his point of view.

The phrase, "Like a son to me," now carried powerful feelings for me. While I felt he was like a father to me, I knew that, over the years, I hadn't acted like a son. I had sent a few cards and letters, but I felt that I could have done more. I had left Ebenezer with the sense that I had been given far more than I gave, and I carried away a great treasure in my heart.

What had it meant to take a white man into his house for a summer, to share his home, his food, and his space when the tension between races was mounting disconcertingly? Probably it was the first time he had opened his life to a white man, in that degree of intimacy. One joyful breakfast had followed another and often dinners turned into little banquets with steaks I had brought home for him, and homemade peach ice cream that I had cranked in the old ice cream freezer. This was just the way I had done things, and I thought little of it. It had never occurred to me that I was having an effect on Daddy King's life.

I suppose I rarely thought of things like that, being more concerned with making a good impression. It was hard for me to realize that the heart of this man whom I revered so much could be touched by small acts of kindness, or that he might be vulnerable, too. I am afraid I was living life more like a man set out to accomplish goals than as one for whom relationships were important. I fear that I missed much of the deeper richness in our experience together.

Now, many years later, Daddy King in the middle of his sermon had dropped this one sentence into my heart. That phrase alone resounded in my ears; it was all I recall from our subsequent conversation, all that moved me during our thanks and farewells. Could it have been that he had come to Cornell in part to tell me that, to thank me for being a human being in a white man's flesh, for crossing the racial divide to be with him? For treating him as if he were like a father, the father I had lost in my adolescence? When a young man has lost his father, he searches the world for a father's blessing, and all at once, I heard words in that unusual moment that carried a measure of that blessing to me.

The years rolled by and Ebenezer was never far from my heart. In 1983 I took my family to visit Daddy King at his home. The oak tree I had planted in gratitude for spending the summer with him was now a large tree, casting beautiful shade across his lawn. He was not strong, and as he walked he needed support. Sparkling with his vibrant spirit, however, he greeted us warmly. As we stood under the oak tree, I took him aside. Remembering his words, which had so often come into my mind and strengthened my heart, I said, "Rev King, you have been like a father to me. Thank you." He paused, and looked out over the roof tops of the houses next door. "Thank you, Brewster, ya hear?" We were quickly joined by my family and we all went inside.

He died a few months after our visit, and as I was unfortunately committed, I could not return for his funeral. His death was a major loss for me.

In the late 1980s, I visited Atlanta and Ebenezer several times again. I took high school and college students, teachers, my wife and children to relive the Freedom Rides. We visited some of the major sites of the civil rights movement — Selma, Birmingham, and Montgomery — before we ended our journey at the Martin Luther King Jr. Center in Atlanta for the conference it gave on nonviolence and the pursuit of justice. My wife, Martha, and I returned to Ebenezer for a reunion celebration in which the church was honoring clergy who had served there. A highlight was our visit with Lillian, with whom we had stayed many years before. She was very elderly, but had the same wonderful laugh and the same extraordinary memory for details. And very special, too, was our visit with Sarah, who has remained close to us over the years.

It takes very little for that deep river to spring forth onto the surface and fill me with emotion. Then I feel like grabbing the pulpit and shouting, as Dr. King shouted, "Let justice roll down like waters..." and listen for the people to shout back to me in chorus, "Amen," "Preach it, Brewster," "Tell it like it is, brother," "Thank you, Jesus," "Make it plain, Brewster." Part of me still wants to live that life and hear again the voice of Daddy King shouting from the congregation, "Preach it, Brewster. Make it plain." Part of who I came to be was formed back then, and I would love to return to those formative days. The mountains and valleys of my inner being still hold that music deep within me, and I know that there are hymns and freedom songs that are crying out to be sung in the sanctuaries and in the streets, in celebration of freedom and justice, and as inspiration for new movements waiting to be born.

Perhaps one of the tragedies of my life is that the river has run so deep that it is not constantly bubbling on the surface. But then, a river finds its bed and over time holds to its course. I was fortunate to have been swept along amid the quiet calms and the thundering turbulences of a mighty river, such as moved Amos a long time ago, and that welled up again with Rosa Parks in December of 1955, and with Dr. King in that same year and for the remaining years of his short life. The son learned from his father, and then the father learned from his son. Within this mighty stream Daddy King kept moving forward, a man knowing pain and tragedy, but still filled with gratitude, love, and hope. We sing and we cry, as we look into the eyes of children or see a tear slowly make its way down the wrinkles of an aged face, and taking our harps down from the tree, we cry and we sing again.

I bless those people who made real for me the vision and the hope for a new world. I bless those people who led me to that place from which there is no turning back.